DESTA MEANS JOY

Dr. Desta Langena Letta

DEDICATION

As my autobiography is written, I was contemplating to whom I would dedicate this book. I decided not to address one person or one group only, but I must mention key people and group who have directly and indirectly influenced, impacted and shaped my life and ministry journey. To list some: (1) Mrs. Gowan who was burdened to the lost people of dark Africa, so that she labored in her day and night prayers for sub-Sahara Africa countries, that I am the product of her prayers and labor for mission. (2) To Walter Gowan (Mrs. Gowan's son), Thomas Kent and Rowland Bingham the first SIM pioneer missionaries to Africa in 1893, who sacrificed everything including their life (Walter and Kent died in few months after landing on the soil of Africa) and an extreme attempt and commitment of Bingham to reach the lost in Africa . (3) To all of the first band of pioneer missionaries led by Dr. Lambie in 1928 to plant the first seed of the Gospel in Southern and Western Ethiopia, whose labor made today's southern Ethiopian region to be belt of Ethiopian Evangelical Christianity. (4) The consecutive SIM missionaries who founded Durame Teza mission compound and worked at this station, to mention some: Clarence Duff, John Philips, Ralph Jacobson, Gustav Kayser, John Campbell, David. Mai, Jongeword, Betty Warhanic and other SIM missionaries who have created an extraordinary impact on mine and many Kambattan Christians' and Churches spiritual growth. (5) The three "Gospel Giants" of Kambatta and Hadiya Kale Heywet Church: Abagole (from Dubancho), Abay Edamo (from Ashira),Helam Segaro (from Mishigida) who labored day and night for the salvation of the lost from the first day of their conversion until their last breath. These pillars and others laid unshakable foundation of the gospel legacy in this region. (6) My biological mother Arfichie who dedicated me to the Lord after my birth, who invested everything for children especially on me for our spiritual and physical healthy growth. (7) Howard Brant, John Kayser and Tim, Jacobson, Rick Calenberg has changed my total outlook on global missions. My direct connection with them and their dynamic input on my life played and also still playing an extraordinary role on my missionary journey. At the last not the least, I dedicate this book to many countless brothers and sisters in Christ those who have positively impacted my spiritual life and ministerial journey.

Recommendations

Desta means joy...and he is both a joy and joyful. Like David the Psalmist, he has an intensity of soul like few you may ever meet. On the same day you may hear him roaring in laughter at something funny or weeping in prayer. He is without doubt a "chosen vessel" ... passionately mobilizing the church and calling people to prayer for the nations of the world. His story is a unique example to us all.

Dr. Howard Brant: Formerly Deputy International Director, SIM International.

Reading the stories of great missionary heroes of the past has been a passion of mine. But one of the greatest blessings of my life getting to know and befriend a modern missionary hero, Desta Langena. His joyful love for the Lord and people, his prayer life, and his ministry as the visionary leader of AIPM, have all challenged me as a missionary and teacher of missions. And joining the thousands of believers in worship on Mt. Ambaricho is one of the highlights of my life. In short, Desta Langena is my missionary hero and I am thrilled that his story is now available in this perfectly titled book, Desta Means Joy. More than joy, it will bring you to praise of the God who has used this man in our generation and to a strong conviction to engage in bold and sacrificial prayer that God will raise up more Desta's in Ethiopia and beyond for the harvest that still remains.

Dr. Rick Calenberg: Former Professor of Missions and Intercultural Studies, Dallas Theological Seminary and current President of the Evangelical Seminary of West Africa, Monrovia, Liberia.

What a wonderful story of God's work in and through the life of Dr. Desta Letta! It's not only inspirational, but it also provides a model for revival and missions. I was so blessed by Dr. Desta's humble faith, heart for his people, and faith to launch a mission's movement among his people. What a challenge! Everyone needs to read the chapter describing how a prayer movement turned into a missions movement. I believe it shows us God's method for reaching the world for Jesus. Thank you, Dr. Desta for sharing your story! I hope that believers around the world will read it and be blessed and inspired to attempt great things for God!

Dr. Sammy Tippit, Author and International Evangelist

This is the thrilling account of how God transformed Desta Langena Letta and the Kambatta people group of Ethiopia from demon possession to a missionary sending dynamo. It's an amazing account of how God directed a group of people out of darkness into light, out of hopelessness to purposeful, eternal life. The reader will be greatly blessed.

David Mai, retired missionary to Ethiopia

I was introduced to Dr. Desta in 2006, when I served at EKSM on a short term mission trip. On January 19th of that year, I climbed to the top of Mt. Ambaricho to pray with 80,000 others for world missions. This experience changed my life forever. Desta Means Joy is an amazing account of how God used Dr. Desta to help reach the lost in Ethiopia and beyond, building God's kingdom. You will be richly blessed when you read this book.

Robert Hogarth. AIPM USA Board Chairman

CONTENTS

Foreword

Missions used to be all about sending missionaries "from the West to the rest!" But in our generation, the tide has shifted and God is raising up missionary movements from all over the world. The story you are about to read chronicles the birth of one of these amazing non-western missions.

The story is special because it recounts the phenomenal story of its founder, Desta Langena. It is special because it shows how an indigenous mission society, was ignited from the torch carried by faithful men and women from the West. Those early missionaries believed that if the churches they planted were self-propagating, self-governing and self-funded... that one day indigenous missions would spring up on African, Asian and Latin American soil. This story is a vindication of their vision.

It is also a story of God's hand upon a chosen vessel. I have been to where Desta was born. He told me about how his mother, who was involved with the occult had lost several of her children before him. When he was about to be born, she called for the evangelists—was gloriously delivered and saved and then gave birth to Desta, meaning joy! And what a joy he is. I remember the first time we met. He was chosen as one of 10 Ethiopians we were taking to India as the first missionaries ever sent by their home churches to another part of the world. I specifically remember one night when we started telling jokes. I have never heard anyone laugh so freely and heartily as Desta did that night. No wonder he is called "Joy."

That hilarious spirit, however, could not disguise a very deep spirituality. This book tells about the torture he endured during the communist years. When I asked him about it years later, he told me that he does not like to talk much about it...lest others would think of him as some kind of spiritual giant...and he didn't want to be idolized.

When our team got to India, he was assigned to work with one of the local Indian pastors. Immediately he asked for a place to pray. As you will see, prayer is a huge part of Desta's life. The pastor told him to pray in the church. So early on Friday morning, Desta would go to the Indian church and kneel down on the floor and begin praying out loud as is the custom of many Ethiopians. People passing by said, "There is a mad man in our church calling on his gods in a language we do not know." Later they learned that Desta was a man of God... and his prayers were going to the God of Heaven. One day, a woman who was a prayer warrior herself passed by. She thought "If this man comes all the way from Africa and prays in my Indian church, why should I not join him?" Not knowing what he was praying, she knelt down beside him. Others saw what was happening and before our time in India was complete, there were 70 people joining Desta in his Friday prayers.

When our team returned from India, we visited the home churches of each of its ten members. In Ethiopian culture, one should not brag about their achievements... or at least it is viewed that way. But as their leaders, we could tell of the amazing things that these men had done in India. We would gather all the elders together and I would tell their stories. On a number of occasions, Desta stood up and announce... "Now we will take an offering for foreign missions." This had not been done before in any of the churches. Frankly there we not missionaries to go...but this was seed money for the future.

Suddenly dozens of people were rising up out of their seats and coming forward with money in hand. It was collected on a large mat and at the end the tally was given. It was then, that my own eyes were opened to how God could move on the hearts of those from the non-affluent nations of the world. The secret was in their large numbers, and in their generosity. Some gave one and five Birr denominations...but there were hundreds of such offerings. Others stood to say they would give a month's worth of their salary. Everywhere we went the story was the same. All this was just a precursor or what would happen as Desta formed his indigenous mission.

I met with the first board of the Ambaricho Prayer and Mission Movement. They asked me to be an honorary member. I was so honored. Before I left that meeting, they asked if they could pray for me. As they prayed, I felt someone down at my feet holding my ankles. My feet were being blessed to take the Gospel around the world. It was the spirit of Ambaricho.

I have been on the prayer mountain with Desta several times. The vastness of the crowd is overwhelming. I will never forget the crowd being challenged to face north, south, east and west as they lifted their hands and called out the names of the countries for which they were praying... Sudan...Mongolia...Uruguay... Iceland...China...Somalia. They were literally praying for the nations of the world. As they prayed, I saw an old man praying not far from the podium. I could understand his language so I drew close to hear his prayer. "Dear Lord, I have a large family and cannot go. But please, take one of my children to the ends of the earth and let them tell the Gospel to people who have never heard."

I count it a very high honor to have known and been a close friend of Desta Langena for over twenty years. My prayer is that this abbreviated story of his life and ministry will bless you. I pray that God will continue to use the work that Desta has started for His glory...and for the expansion of the Gospel around the world until Jesus comes and we stand before His throne...people from every nation, tribe and tongue.

Dr. Howard Brant
SIM-Deputy International Director Emeritus
Renton, WA – April 18, 2018

ACKNOWLEDGMENTS

I want to give first and foremost praises and all the glory to God to Almighty who has chosen me before the foundation of this world, saved me through the precious blood of Jesus Christ His son. He is the only One who has enabled and sustained me to serve Him. It is only "by His grace I am what I am" (1 Cor. 15:9-10), not by my strength or any ability. The story in this book is His story, so that He deserves to receive all the praises and glory for what He has done in my life and ministry journey.

I want to say thank you to David and Darlene Mai who labored day and night in writing this book. Their dedication, focus and perseverance many years in collecting information, writing and rewriting is beyond expression. Mainly the way Mr. Mai selected important titles for each Chapters, organizing in wonderful order how this story would be meaningful and understandable by English language Speakers and readers.

I want to say thank you the Clackamas Bible Church editorial group who have dedicated and invested their time for many months in editing the whole document of this book.

I want say thank you to my wife and children who have sacrificed a lot whenever I left for US spending months for writing this book and other ministries. Their patience, love and encouragement has been a great deal in bringing this book to reality

I want to say thank you to my Father (who is currently with the Lord), my Mom (who is still alive), all my siblings who have invested a lot in helping my growth, shaping my life and sacrificing their everything for the wellbeing of my personal life and ministry, who have contributed the lion share in my yesterday's, today's and tomorrow's life and ministry. I want to thank Bob Hogarth who has done an extraordinary contribution for this book to be printed and available in the hands of readers.

I want to thank all my brothers and sisters in Christ those who live all over the world who have encouraged me, supported me, prayed for me, taught me god line.

Introduction

In each person's life God has divine plan, which is true in my personal life and ministry too. Though my distressed parents did not have any clue what would happened and come out of a boy who was born at the period of spiritual darkness, misery in the family and our nation, God designed to bring me forth from this particular family and to this planet according to His divine purpose. It reminds me the great affliction period of Israel in Egypt (Exodus 1) that made them to cry desperately before God (Exodus 2). As an answer to their prayer, He prepared and called a man named Moses to deliver them out of their existing desperate situation (Exodus 2,3). Moses' birth, growth and preparation has similar picture to my personal life, as Stephen the martyr, stated in the book of Acts.

"But when the time of the promise drew near, which God had sworn to Abraham, the people grew and multiplied in Egypt, till another king arose, who knew not Joseph. This man dealt treacherously with our people, and oppressed our forefathers, making them expose their babies, so they might not live. At this time Moses was born and was well pleasing to God; and he was brought up in his father's house three months. But when he was set out, Pharaoh's daughter took him up, and brought him up as her own son." (Acts 7:17-21) NKJ)

In the same way the life of Moses was spared, God also spared my life so many times from the Devil's plotted and vicious killing plans. Also, as Moses grew up in the Palace of Pharaoh with education and wisdom, God also prepared me through different trials of life and educational trainings. As God also prepared Moses in the wilderness for forty years teaching him humility and perseverance, God also allowed so many odd experiences to shape my character for the purpose He has in my life and plans He designed for me. Many challenges I underwent prepared me for the great battle with the enemy, my flesh and this world in the years to come.

Surprisingly I never had courage to take any challenge that God had been bringing to my ways. He challenged me to stand strong in the middle of storms, asked me to leave my job, directed me to go places I am totally afraid of, to say no for prestigious positions offered and many others. The following biblical text about Moses was a great challenge that brought me to my knees to plead before God for help.

*By faith Moses, when he was come to years, **refused to be called** the son of Pharaoh's daughter; **Choosing rather to suffer** affliction with the people of God, **than to enjoy the pleasures of sin for a season;** Esteeming the reproach of Christ greater riches than the treasures in Egypt: for he had respect unto the recompense of the reward. By faith he forsook Egypt, not fearing the wrath of the king: for he endured, as seeing him who is invisible" (Heb. 11:24-27) KJ.*

Even though the above passage persistently compelling to take step of faith, I found it out to be very difficult. But God did not let me go with my arguments and excuses, rather He reminded me His word.

*"Come to Me, ... **Take my yoke upon you, and learn of Me**, for I am gentle and lowly in heart, and you will find rest for your souls" (Matt. 11:28, 29) NKJ.*

Therefore, every step of faith was full of constant battle and struggle with myself, my family, my church and even my nation's ideology. But in each step I saw God intervening as I decided to obey His leading. In the midst of painful journey, I saw Him always at my side. Therefore, *"Desta Means Joy"* book reveals you how my life was full of ups and downs, picks and pits but incredibly polished through many encounters in life journey: - my trials, family, peer group, school mates, workplace friends and ministry comrades.

A great person who played the greatest role in my life is my mother a woman of integrity and honesty as a Christian, honest wife and great mother. As Mary was watching out at her Son, Jesus, my mom also had special attention on me than her other children, because of the vison she saw from Jesus at one night. He appeared to her and told her: - "His name is Desta (Joy) and He will be my servant." Amazingly enough she had never told me this until I came to hear from her just recently after my 60th birthday. My mom's strong discipline, deep love, and direction to love Jesus and walk with Him were pivotal in my overall life journey. My hard-working father and godly siblings were also great part in my upbringing.

Also, my journey with my life partner Zenebech for the last 30 years and my five dear children (age of 30 to 22 by now) who labored with me in the cause of the God's Kingdom work incredible place in my life and ministry. They had been great blessing beyond my expression. I always say that if God had not prepared this dearly lady (my wife) to my life what would my life and ministry look like? My lovely children had never complained about missing their dad who is always on board for ministry from their early age till now. But God is so good, and He knows how He orchestrates everything for His Name's sake and for the furtherance of His Kingdom.

The hardships I faced with Christians through the fire of persecution during the communist regime of Ethiopia (1974-1991), brought me much closer to God and matured in my faith and ministry. God by His power protected I and my companions who faced the challenge of that persecution, from many planned assassinations by communist leaders though many of us were thrown in prison and being tortured severely for the love of our dear Savior. The greatest lessons we have learned during this period was that our loyalty and commitment to the Word of God, extraordinary prayer life and consecrated living... became our three outstanding spiritual foundations those sustained us in the midst of severe suffering.

I want to mention some of key people in my life, because, these people had played an extraordinary role in shaping my spiritual walk with the Lord and ministry. God brought them for a great purpose to my life used them as part of my spiritual growth and ministry. The following are few words about them. But the readers can get be acquainted with them as they read the book how these people and others positively impacted my life and ministry.

David Mai (PK – pastor's kid), SIM missionary to Durame, Ethiopia. He was used by God to disciple and prepare me for the future ministry and for coming persecution of Ethiopian communism (1974-1991). He played an immense role at my early age, not only from his biblical teachings, but also from his personal life and an extraordinary commitment for ministry and work.

Tim Jacobson (MK- missionary kid), the son of pioneer missionary to Durame, named Ralph and Doris became my mentor. It was trough him God worked out everything in leading me to the calling God gave me long ago, "to the mission work" I am currently involving nationally and globally.

John Kayser (MK), the son of Gustav and Lois Kayser (Pioneer missionaries and coworkers with Ralph Jacobson). God used John Kayser to help me understand what missions is all about. His extreme dedication for God's call challenged me to be faithful for the Great commission. He is like my big brother and I as his younger brother. God opened the door for me to study Missions in Singapore. He was always next to me in my missiology training in Singapore, and God used Him to establish of Ethiopian Kale Heywet School of Missions (EKSM). Also in many occasions we both were together at many missions conferences and consultations which brought amazing understanding and foundation in my missiological understanding and over all my missionary endeavor.

Howard Brant (MK- Missionary Kid)- has great part in my missionary involvement and journey. He is truly my spiritual father. Especially his great reputation in Ethiopian church played dynamic role in bringing Ethiopian church from nowhere to somewhere which I discussed in this book. I always saw him standing next me encouraging and guiding me. He always brought me closer to Him as Jesus did to Apostle John. He was my ever mentor as missiologist, Bible teacher, church and mission leader, not only in the past but now and then.

Rick Calenberg, was mightily used by God in bringing me to the Western Seminary for my further studies. Beyond my education, he poured his life and shared everything he had on me during my stay here in the states. We were like apostle Paul (him) and his disciple Timothy (I). We both traveled so many places in the United States, and as we travelled we shared so many heart felts together.

The pioneers to Ethiopia those who came especially to Durame, like Ralph Jacobson, Gustav Kayser and John Campbell, and Albert Brant (a missionary to Shashamanie and Gedeo) people have impacted my life and ministry in countless manners. They laid unshakable foundation to early church in 1960s, and 1970s, especially the Kambatta and Gedeo, which directly and indirectly impacted my life. Currently the Kambatta tribe (people group) is more than 95% evangelical Christians, that he Kambattan Church is an amazing mission minded church.

The testimony of these pioneer missionaries have been ringing at my ear for many years, which caused me to pray earnestly saying:- "Oh God would you use me like these pioneers, that I would be used to change my nation, my continent and reach the world like these godly men and women who have impacted my nation with the Gospel message." Thankfully I met Ralph and Doris Jacobson at their house in Vancouver Canada before their home going.

Also I met John Campbell before his home going. I met Mrs. Kayser (who is still alive) and Mrs. Brant before she went home. I received their blessings through their prayers, which I consider myself as one of the most blessed people in the world, because I am shaped by such godly and great people, because of their such investment on me.

Therefore, the story written in this book is about me "DESTA MENS JOY," but it is truly "THEIR STORY," more than my story, because they were the people whom God has prepared before the foundation of the earth. They have contributed and played an enormous role not only in shaping my life and ministry, but also in an emergence and growth of Ethiopian Kale Heywet School of Missions (EKSM) and Ambaricho International Prayer and Missions Movement (AIPM).

You will be amazed as you dive reading pages of this book "how God raises a weak and inadequate vessel and choose to bring glory to His name and to further His Kingdom." The following text of the Bible passage of Apostle Paul reflects a clear picture of my journey in the past, present and for the years to come in the future.

*For I am the least of the apostles, who am not worthy to be called an apostle, ... But **by the grace of God I am what I am**: and his grace which was bestowed upon me was not in vain; but **I labored ... yet not I, but the grace of God which was with me** (1 Cor. 15:9,10).*

Enjoy Reading!

Dr. Desta Langena Letta, Founder and Director of AIPM

Chapter One

Synopsis

Desta Means Joy is an account of a grassroots movement of God's Spirit among a group of Christians in southern Ethiopia for the cause of world evangelization. The account is told by the main character, Desta Langena in the first person and written by SIM missionary David Mai one of the missionaries used by God in the discipling of this humble servant.

The account begins during the years communism ruled Ethiopia (1974-1991).

Chapter Two: Perilous Days, introduces the reader to a courageous young Ethiopian Christian, Desta Langena, whose faith is tested in the crucible of persecution at the hands of communist cadres. Haile Selassie, the benevolent Emperor of Ethiopia (1930-1974), used by God to open Ethiopia to missions, had been deposed and lost his life. The missionaries had subsequently been made to leave. God used this dark period in Ethiopia's history to develop the faith of Desta and many other Ethiopian Christians, preparing them for the work of missions as part of His plan to get the gospel to the ends of the earth at the end of the age.

Chapter Three: A Father's Struggle For His Son's Survival, goes back to the beginning of Desta's life. It tells how Ato (Mr.) Langena, Desta's father, was used by God to preserve Desta's life when Satan did his best to snuff it out at its inception. The accuracy of this part of the account is not assured because it was written after Ato Langena passed away. But it is factual in most aspects and tells how God spared Desta's life.

Chapter Four: From Darkness to Light, is a detailed account of how the gospel came to the Kambatta people, Desta's tribal people, and the three other tribes in southern Ethiopia that have been most receptive to the gospel. It is a thrilling chapter in the history of modern missions in the nineteenth and twentieth centuries.

Chapter Five: The Church Matures, is still part of the history that provides insight into the life of this servant of God. It tells how God's Word was planted deeply in the lives of the Kambattans by two of God's choice servants and their mates. Ralph Jacobson rode his mule, Alganesh (she is my bed), to provide Bible training to Kambattan church leaders who, because of family responsibilities, could not be a part of the resident Bible School on the mission compound. Gus Kayser ran the Bible School and prepared the notes that were used in all the teaching. During these years, the 1950s and 60s, the mimeograph machine was never idle in Kambatta. These two men, gifted and empowered by God's Spirit, wove God's Word deeply into the fabric of the Kambatta people.

It was during this time of maturing that God brought a third dedicated servant and his wife to the Kambatta Church in the person of John Campbell and his wife, Marj. He established academic education throughout the area. The Emperor, Haile Selassie, had only two requirements of mission organizations that wanted to preach the gospel in his country. They must establish a school grades 1-4 and a medical clinic. When John arrived many of the Kambattans had completed grade 4, so it was agreed that as the Church was able to take the responsibility for a lower grade, the mission (SIM) would add an upper grade. At the end of John's time in Ethiopia (health needs of family) the church was doing grades 1-6 and the SIM was doing grades 7-10. This is the setting of Chapter Five.

Chapter Six: Reunited, relates how Desta became a Christian and a scholar. The Holy Spirit knows that it takes both to lead a missions movement in a third world country in today's world. God equips His servants for the work He calls them to do!

Chronologically, Chapter Two comes now between Chapters Six and Seven. So, if the readers wanted the narrative to flow, they could re-read chapter one before going on to Chapter Six

Chapter Seven: The University and My First Job, is Desta telling what a pleasant surprise and refuge his university training turned out to be. Upon receiving his bachelor's degree in physics, Desta was assigned to teach physics at the Teachers' Training Institute in Bale Robe. The next nine years were an adventure in a place three days travel from his home by public transport. It became evident why God took Desta to this post. It was devoid of churches and over those years God used Desta to establish seven churches along with his responsibilities as a physics instructor. This experience was one more part of the training Desta would need to become the director of a mission organization which would major in evangelism, church planting, and training church leaders.

Chapter Eight: Romance and Family, took place during the same period in Desta's life as Chapter Six. It tells how God provided a wife for His servant. It is a warm and wonderful example of how God works, sensing and providing the needs of His children.

Chapter Nine: Dark-skinned People Can Be Missionaries, tells how God showed Ethiopians that they did not need white skin to qualify them to serve as missionaries. A change in the education policy of Ethiopia brought Desta back to Durame High School in his home area because instruction was to be done in the local dialects. For the next three years Desta taught physics at DHS and God used him as an agent for revival in the Kambatta churches by teaching mainly on prayer. Desta was selected by the national Kale Heywet Office (Desta's denomination) as one of two men sent to Bethany School of Missions (BSM) in Singapore to receive training in missions. There he developed a lasting friendship with John Kayser, son of Gus and Lois Kayser and principal of the School of Missions. Upon his return to Ethiopia Desta was chosen by Howie Brant to be one of the ten Ethiopian men sent to India as short term missionaries. All of these experiences were being used by God to prepare Desta to become the founder and director of Ambaricho International Prayer and Missions Movement (AIPM).

Chapter Ten: Reunited! is the amazing account of how Desta and the scribe for this book were reunited after 29 years. David Mai and his family followed the John Campbell family to serve the Kambatta Church as education specialists. David had a master's degree in teaching science and Luci, his wife, had her masters in math. They were in charge of the school grades 7 thru 10 that Desta attended. David offered extra discipleship classes and other challenges to the student body of 450 students. Desta embraced every challenge and the student and his teacher became close friends. Now in God's sovereign plan that friendship would be rekindled. It resulted in Desta getting his doctorate in Missiology and David becoming chairman of the AIPM USA Board and scribe for this book.

Chapter Eleven: A Prayer Movement Becomes a Missions Movement, is the account of how God changed a prayer movement into an Ethiopian missionary training and sending agency through the seed money provided by seven young girls and boys.

Chapter Twelve: The Sanbatte Shalla Story, tells how God called one of Desta's brothers, Tamiru, to become the first AIPM missionary and how God used this loving servant to break through the powerful invisible walls of resistance in this stronghold of Islam.

Chapter Two

Perilous Days

July 9, 1978 was a sad day for me and many others who loved the missionaries who lived and labored among us. These dedicated, caring teachers were being deported by the new leaders in our country. Emperor Haile Selassie had been overthrown and the communists under the leadership of Mengistu Haile Mariam, head of the military government, were now in control.

The communist leaders had come to the Tezza Mission Compound. Three miles from my hometown of Durame. at the foot of Mt. Ambaricho, the Tezza compound was the location of our school. The missionaries were ordered to leave. They were unceremoniously sent away with the clothes on their backs and what could be carried in a suitcase. Leaving their vehicles and the rest of their belongings behind, the missionaries walked the eight miles to the nearest public transportation.

What was happening was no surprise. The mission had closed the academic school the previous year because of the insubordination of some student instigators who had been indoctrinated in communist ideology. Even that was under the control of the Sovereign of the universe because it gave me a chance to enroll in the Bible school on the mission compound since there was no longer an academic school for me to attend!

That year in Bible school was crucial in my preparation for the horrendous treatment that awaited me at the hands of the communists. Mr. Ted Kayser was my main teacher that year. He had been a civil engineer before he became a Christian and felt God's call to be a missionary. His godly grandfather spoke into his life when it was steeped in godless, evolutionary science with the question, "Was you there?" God used this simple question to start Mr. Kayser on a journey that led to the foot of the cross where God lifted the burden of a life of slavery to Satan, sin and death in exchange for the gift of eternal abundant life in Christ.

Mr. Kayser really knew what he was talking about and he taught his students many wonderful things. He told us that true science is in agreement with the Bible and that the science that disagrees with the Bible is false. He taught a wonderful course on the books of Daniel and Revelation. He gave us many insights into communist ideology. In addition to being atheistic, he told us that communism denies life after death and that it also teaches that men will usher in utopia on earth. We learned many things about the underground church in Russia, Bulgaria, Romania and China and how it functions under a repressive communist-controlled government. Without that year of Bible school I would have been ill-equipped for what followed.

After the missionaries were forced to leave, and with that year under Mr. Kayser's instruction, I enrolled in eleventh grade. I attended the government school in Durame, a town of 50,000 which though being located only three miles from my village was under a different local government and under different communist leaders. During that year I went to my home only a few times per month and stayed only a little while because the communist leaders in my village were looking for me. I had been purposely avoiding the youth movement meetings where Ethiopian youths were being indoctrinated. They were made to read the writings of Karl Marx and Fredrick Engels, German socialist leaders and theoreticians, and about Lenism and the Bolshevik Revolution in Russia.

The spokesmen for communism made statements that raised red flags in my mind. One such statement was the slogan "ABIYOT KEHULU BELLAY NAW." In English this means, "The revolution is above all." This slogan was everywhere. It was repeated frequently on the radio and TV. All government meetings such as the youth indoctrination classes opened and closed with this slogan. Placards of this slogan were plastered everywhere. I knew it was wrong because John 3:31 says: "He who comes from above (Jesus) is above all". I feared what would happen to my beloved Ethiopia if we exchanged the truth for a lie.

Another such slogan was "TEFETIRON BEKUTITIR SIR INADERGALIN" for which the English equivalent is, "We are in control of (can subdue) nature." God says in Colossians that Jesus created all things and holds all things together. Such lies I feared would cause Ethiopians to forget God and fall prey to Satan. Again communism taught people to hate their enemies and curse them. I was convinced that such teaching was against the Bible and would not benefit our nation.

There was much propaganda against the West and against America. This did not ring true with me because I knew of all the good the missionaries from the United States, Canada, Great Britain and Australia had done for my people. They planted indigenous churches, built schools and clinics and even hospitals, as well as provided clean water and introduced improved seed for the farmers. When famine came to the land, the church and mission leaders organized the peaceful and equitable distribution of grain sent to our country by charitable organizations and governments around the world.

All of these alarm bells going off in my mind made me feel very uncomfortable and kept me away from the youth indoctrination classes. This caused the communist leaders to be suspicious. They questioned my family many times and assigned people to be on the look-out for me. They told them to immediately notify the village police so that I could be apprehended. Fortunately, the local communist leaders could not go to areas outside their jurisdiction and make arrests. Because of this I was protected by God for some time.

My offenses were being absent from the indoctrination classes on Saturdays and the development project work on Sundays. These projects consisted of road and bridge building. I was always occupied Saturdays with choir practice, Bible study and prayer with fellow Christians. Sundays I would attend services, sing in the choir and preach. I was one of the main preachers among the choir members. The youth in this choir read books like Richard Wurmbrand's *Tortured for Christ* and *The Catacombs*. We also studied a commentary on Joshua, a wonderful treatise on possessing the land and spiritual warfare. These books gave us awareness about the reality of communism and equipped us for the suffering which we were going to face in the near future.

It was truly a cat and mouse game between me and the communist cadres from my home area. They scheduled classes and work days on Saturday and Sunday to take young people out of the life and work of the church, and I was busy those two days not in my home church but in other churches four or five hours from my home.

As an aside, it was during those fellowship times on the weekends that I became better acquainted with Zenebech, a lovely young lady two years behind me in school. We often talked together, and I sensed that she looked up to me as an older, more mature Christian brother that she could confide in and find answers to her questions pertaining to the Bible and Christian living. I have to admit that I really enjoyed our times together.

Since I had to stay away from home, Ato Seratu and Wizero Amarech opened their home and their church to me. Ato Seratu was an energetic coffee farmer and trader and one of the main elders in the Durame #2 Kale Heywet Church located right in front of his house. Their house was like a refugee camp for me and my dear prayer companions Tadesse Yohanness and Elias Handisso. Wizero Amarech was a very lovely, gracious woman and a wonderful cook. I don't know what I would have done without the hospitality of this wonderful Christian family during my eleventh and twelfth grade years.

Ayelech Wadajo, an amazing young woman of prayer who was zealous for holiness, greatly impacted my personal and prayer life. She had been in Yergallem for schooling where she grew strong in her faith through the Christian youth movement. She helped me grow in my faith and helped strengthen me spiritually for what was ahead. There were many close Christian friends who greatly impacted my spiritual life at this time. To list only a few of them they were Tesfanesh Yohannes, Beriso Lodebo, Kebebush Atebo, Abebech and Aster Mikore, Simeon Dana, Yohannes Bassana, Abraham Babanto, Bizunesh Hadero, Desta and Tesfaye Wanore, Semerew Seso, Zenebech Markos, Aregesh Bafa, Yonas Abo, Eyasu Abuye, Almaz Abuye, and my younger brother Abebe Langena and his friends Matewos, Indrias and Ayele.

I had just finished eleventh grade and returned to my home area. I was only home for a short time when the authorities caught me and took me into custody. As I look back I guess I was thinking that by that time they would have forgotten about me and my absence from their meetings and work days. That proved to be wishful thinking.

After the Communist officials questioned me, they ascertained that I had serious reservations about what was going on in the country and put me in the local prison. For three weeks they interrogated me. They were trying to find things for which to accuse me. I was not in agreement with cursing my enemies, that men can control nature, and that the revolution is above all. I was, however, willing to fight for my country. At that time Somalia in the east was fighting against Ethiopia. Eritrean rebels in the north and young people who wanted Chinese communism in the capital city, Addis Ababa, were also fighting Mengistu's government. Since the Bible teaches us to accept our authorities as from God, I had no intention of being a part of a rebellion against the central government.

I was an enigma to my captors. On-the-one-hand, I was not wanting to fight against the central government, in fact, I was willing to fight against their enemies. However, I was firmly entrenched in Christian teachings which taught the importance of individual responsibility and appeared to be linked to capitalism, whereas communism is socialistic. Also, biblical Christianity believes in life after death while communism denies life after death, and asserts that man can usher in utopia on earth.

The communist authorities in my local area tried hard to get me to repeat their slogans. They even sent church people to reason with me. These people advised me that to recite the slogans which were contrary to the Bible was not the same as disowning Jesus. I could not agree with them.

Since I would not change my mind after three weeks they sent me to the main prison in Durame. There the communist guards greatly increased the pressure on me to renounce my Lord. My joy in finding Jesus Christ as my personal Savior nine years earlier was under serious attack. Besides the rats and foul food, I was beaten daily not only by the guards but also by other prisoners who had sold out to communism but were in prison for other offenses. They were given permission by the guards to do so. My only crimes were that I refused to recite their slogans and to stop speaking about Jesus. All of them were trying to break me, but the sovereign Lord was strengthening me day by day. I was prepared to perish under their hands but God had other plans for me, and I was unexpectedly released from that prison of continual torture after two months and in time to enroll in grade twelve.

Now that you know my life was spared, I will fill in some of the sordid details of those horrible months during that summer between my eleventh and twelfth grade. Even though the period of imprisonment was short, there was almost daily torture by the atheist guards, prisoners, communist cadres and officials. In one incident that sticks in my mind the guard was torturing me for most of the afternoon. I received a minimum of three hundred lashes that day. My back was totally torn up and blood was flowing from the wounds inflicted by the whip. To this day I carry many scars on my back as reminders of that day and others almost as bad. I was unable to sleep for almost a week after that episode. On that same day the same person beat the inside of my foot until it was totally swollen and I was unable to walk.

In another incident another guard was ordered by a communist cadre to torture me on a daily basis. One particular day during which the guard consumed much alcohol and was in a drunken frenzy, he beat my right side with a very thick stick like a mean-spirited African might beat his donkey. I thought all my ribs were broken. But thanks be to God not a single rib was broken. This was an undeniable miracle to me and the other observers who were there that day.

On another day communist party members, who were imprisoned because of some ideological differences with the government leaders, were beating me by the order of the cadres and the guards. They slapped my face with such force that it looked like the face of a prize fighter who had been beaten to a pulp by his opponent.

One day, the head cadre of the district came and ordered me to say, "Communism is above all." But I replied "No, communism is not above all, it is Jesus who is above all." The cadre became so furious that he beat me almost the whole morning until he collapsed from the exertion. After realizing I was firm in my stand, he pointed his gun at my throat planning to kill me. During those days in Ethiopia killing was common for the communists. It was estimated that in Addis Ababa, the capital city of Ethiopia, more than 55,000 people were killed by the communists. I believe it was God's intervention alone that spared my life that day. The cadre did his best to change my mind but God enabled me to stand strong in my faith, honoring God in the midst of suffering. Finally, he ordered his junior cadre who was watching the vicious beating to bring his hands full of dust and force me to eat it. Then the senior cadre laughed and mocked me saying, "You are destined to eat dust and mud - your portion is eating dust! Ha ha ha!"

Even though the torture was unbearable, the grace of God was more than the pain of torture. (I Corinthians 12:9). Praise the Lord! My daily wish was to die for Jesus!!

I was not the only one who was imprisoned for my faith. My friends Taddesse Yohannes, Elias and Aster Handiso, Zeleke Bekele, Eyasu Abuye and others experienced terrible suffering for their faith in that Durame prison.

By His grace and mercy God did not hand our lives over to be killed by the communists. Instead, their torture increased our faith in the Lord and built our spiritual life stronger for our future life and ministry. Continued persecution deepened our love for God, brought us closer to Him and helped us know and serve Him more. During those days of suffering I came to understand the sweetness and transforming power of God's Word, the role of prayer, and the power and work of the Holy Spirit in my personal life. I came to realize that private and corporate prayer is indispensable to the growth of the church and its ministries.

Emperor Haile Sellassie with dignitaries. He allowed the missionaries from North America, Europe, Australia to work in Ethiopia.

Chapter Three

A Father's Struggle For His Son's Survival

Seventeen years before my persecution at the hands of the Communist cadres, when my life was just beginning, my father, Ato Langena, was overwhelmed with worry! His beloved son's (my) life was threatened by the same demonic force that took the lives of two of his daughters. He was filled with anxiety and anguish as he walked along the African trail.

From childhood my mother was troubled by forces of evil. She began to behave strangely after their marriage. When she became pregnant with me she would go on unannounced forays into the dangerous African bush and be lost until she was searched for and brought back.

My father tried everything he knew to deliver my mother from her dangerous behavior but to no avail. He consulted with family members and trusted friends. He made several trips to the local witchdoctors and offered many sacrifices of chickens and lambs to appease the spirits. He even made the four-hour climb to the top of Mt. Ambaricho and the most powerful source of spiritual help he knew of.

Abba Serrecho, the head witchdoctor of the entire Kambatta tribe, lived on that mountain, the tallest in southern Ethiopia. This witchdoctor often had great success in satisfying the requests of his devotees. He was a wealthy man because of the gifts of cattle and other livestock he received from his devotees, being feared and worshipped by them.

Though exhausted from the 9,500 foot ascent to the top of the 10,000 foot mountain, my father had been full of hope. Surely this powerful witchdoctor could affect a change in the erratic behavior that was threatening the life of his wife and his son. Or, perish the thought, would his hopes be dashed by her continued destructive behavior?

She seemed controlled by the same evil force that plagued other women of the tribe and which ended in futility and the tragic, abrupt end to the anticipated joy of an addition to the family. During these days in Ethiopia, unexplainable deaths were common and many youths and adults became deaf and dumb or even blind by this evil, spiritual power. Also the women possessed by this evil power produced children with these handicaps or who were lame or had other deformities. Before the arrival of the gospel to that area, Ato Langena's family line could not eat goat meat without vomiting. Snakes were everywhere. The tribal people felt compelled to feed these reptiles to get relief and earn the favor of these forces of evil.

Ato Langena had heard about the power of this head witchdoctor who would crawl into the cave under Covenant Rock. There the very dangerous huge poisonous serpents licked the butter plastered on his head after which he emerged unscathed and greatly empowered to produce unbelievable feats of spiritual power!

Buoyed by the charisma of the powerful witchdoctor and his incantations, Ato Langena's descent from the mountaintop seemed to pass in no time. However, his hopes were dashed when he arrived home to the news that his wife had again disappeared. She seemed almost hell-bent on destroying her own life and the life of the son recently born to her. This was not like the gentle, beautiful bride he had betrothed just a few years before. She was all he had ever dreamed about--this dignified, highly respected tribesman. What brought about this disturbing, destructive change in his precious sweetheart? It was so unlike her nature to do anything harmful to another of God's creatures, let alone to harm this priceless baby boy. But she seemed incapable of resisting the powerful evil that lurked in the bushes of her soul and threatened to destroy her and her son. "Who will deliver me from the one who seeks my destruction?" she agonized. Yet she was driven as she plunged deeper and deeper into the bush where hyenas stalked their prey and the land was void of water and food and the trails were treacherous. Her life at best was tenuous and at worse close to being snuffed out. Her life flame was like the kuraz (oil lamp) that dimly lit their African hut just before it ran out of kerosene and the flame flickered about to be extinguished.

My father was desperate. This problem was totally out of control and beyond any resources he possessed or could lay hands on. He had never felt so alone, so helpless and unable to find a solution. Being a strong, resourceful man this feeling was totally foreign to him. He was always the one who offered the best answer to problems that threatened to disrupt the sense of well-being and safety in the African bush. As the men of the village pooled their mental and physical prowess to solve a problem it was more often than not he who birthed the ideas that all the others had embraced and implemented with great success. Now, this champion of the people was at a loss to effect a cure for the most important person in his universe--his beloved wife, Arfichie, and to save the life of his son.

As he sat in the smoky darkness of this place he called home, engulfed in hopelessness, exhausted and utterly defeated, an idea brighter than the African sun burst from deep within his soul. Was there really hope for the hopeless? Was there available to this totally despairing human situation, a power that could save this family from the demons that threatened their demise? Could their sealed doom be unsealed at this the eleventh hour? Yet the sense of hope that had flickered to the point of extinction was rapidly growing in the heart of this warrior as he sat in the oppression of total lostness.

It was the talk he had heard about the Jesus people. First, white missionaries, foreigners from a far land, who believed that they had such good news not just for their own tribe but for every tribe in the world that they had left their distant homes and had come to this dark continent with this good news. The talk he had heard in the market and around the evening fire in the village square was that there was victory even over death. This victory was proclaimed in the name of One whose name he had never heard. Jesus, who had lived centuries before in the town of Nazareth in Israel, was the one who had come down to earth from heaven to bring deliverance to all who believed in Him. His death on the cross had paid the price for man's sin so he could be forgiven by God, the benevolent Ruler of the universe and Jesus' Father. This God actually loved people and wanted them to be delivered from all evil. When my father first heard this he quickly dismissed it as too good to be true. But now in his desperation he had nowhere else to turn. This was indeed a strange doctrine yet now it was balm to a tormented, tortured man who had never felt so small.

This Name produced warmth and light in my father's troubled soul. Dare he hope against hope? He had heard rumors about some families in his tribe who had embraced this new doctrine and experienced unimaginable deliverance from all forms of evil.

That settled it! The hope and joy and peace that now washed over his being was something that he had never before experienced. The more he thought about it the more he was convinced that he must seek out these Jesus people and invite them to his compound.

If everything he had tried before was hard, now everything was easy. The first person he asked about contacting the Jesus people knew exactly what he was talking about and to whom he should speak. When he went to the Tezza Church seeking help, Ato Debo and Ato Budugo were very understanding of his problem. They said that they would come to his compound that very Sunday to pray for my mother.

As the two men entered our compound that Sunday afternoon, my agitated mother was walking out the front door of our house leaving me behind in my cradle. Then something amazing happened to her. She was completely delivered from the evil being(s) that had possessed her! The two men shared the gospel with my mother that day and she immediately received the Lord. My mother was a young woman then and now she is over ninety. She gave birth to three more children after me and from that day to this our home has been a very happy home. To express the emotion she experienced that day my mother named me Desta. Desta means joy in Amharic, the trade language of Ethiopia. Not only did joy come to my mother but my father got peace and joy as well. He, too, accepted the good news of abundant, eternal life through faith in Jesus. Praise God my life was miraculously spared that day. He had me in His plans for spreading the gospel in these last days.

My family has been a great blessing in my life. My father and mother loved their children deeply and did not fail to discipline us when we were bad. My father was never afraid to speak the truth even if it included correcting a person of high rank.

My father was a wonderful farmer. He raised a variety of crops such as teff, (grass seed-like grain used to make injera, a large pancake like bread used for dipping in bowls of stew called wat), corn, peas, three kinds of beans, sorghum, millet, barley, wheat, potatoes, sweet potatoes, inset (false banana with edible root), cabbage, limes, bananas and coffee as well as eucalyptus trees. I never knew my father to sell anything in the market except coffee.

He never wanted his family to be without enough to eat. During years of famine I observed my father providing food to relatives and neighbors in need. He passed away in 2009 at the ripe old age of 92.

My mother's brothers really blessed our entire family. They were educated and encouraged the rest of the family to get an education both by their example and financial support. My older brother, Mekonnen, greatly assisted us in this way as well. My older sister, Abebech, blessed our family members with much love and care. My two younger brothers, Abebe and Tamiru, and younger sister, Ejigayehu, are very committed Christians. Ejigayehu has remained single to care for my mother in her old age. Abebe and his wife, Abebech, were much loved missionaries to South Sudan for six years. The people have begged for them to return but Abebech has a physical disability that prevents that. Tamiru was the first Africa International Prayer and Mission Movement (AIPM pronounced I-PAM) [1] missionary whom God used in a mighty way to break the stranglehold of Satan in Sanbatte Shalla. Both these younger brothers have been wonderful disciples of mine and are by my side in spirit even when not in the flesh. I thank God for the blessed family with which he has surrounded me.

Auto Langena and his wife
Aftiche. My father and mother

[1] A grass-roots Ethiopian run missionary training and sending agency.

Chapter Four

From Darkness to Light

My people were held in the clutches of Satan and his minions for more than seven miserable centuries prior to the arrival of Sudan Interior Mission (SIM) missionaries in the late 1920's. What was true of my family was true of everyone of the more than 500,000 tribal members . We were harassed, groping and struggling and in the throes of spiritual darkness and death. My mother was chronically sick and displayed erratic behavior. This sickness and troublesome behavior caused the loss of two baby girls shortly after their birth. It not only robbed our home of these bundles of delight but drove my father to despair. These same oppressive events and similar ones plagued every single hut throughout the area. The women of our tribe not only lost children but they themselves became deaf and dumb or even blind due to demon activity. Adding to the misery, they produced children with these debilitating handicaps or who were lame or had other gross deformities.

Snakes were everywhere! My people were afraid of these creatures, feeding them butter, a precious commodity, and bowing down to them. They believed that more bad things would happen to them if they did not worship and appease these reptiles. Chickens, sheep and oxen were offered to appease spirits. On top of all these were the problems created by intra and extra tribal warfare. The saying, "The way of the transgressor is hard" described us to a "T". Our ancestors worshiped rivers, big trees, rocks and mountains to no avail. My people experienced continual physical and emotional anguish.

What a miserable people we were! Who could free us from this life that was dominated by Satan? The answer to this burning question was on the way in the person of Dr. Thomas Lambie and his party of eleven SIM missionaries. They docked at the Red Sea coastal country of Djibouti. It was Christmas Day of 1927. In keeping with the Christmas Gift of all gifts sent to this sin sick world 2000 years ago in the person of His Son, God was sending the gift of freedom to my people, freedom from the ravages of sin and Satan.

Dr. Lambie led the way. He had already spent seven years in Wollega Province, in the western part of Ethiopia just east of the Sudan border. While there he formed friendships that God was about to use to help gain acceptance for the missionaries to preach the gospel in Ethiopia.

The Lambie team made their way to Addis Ababa, Ethiopia's capital, located in the central highlands. Soon they were headed to Jimma on horseback. The date was March 7, 1928. Setting off from the capital city, the party reached Marako after 4 days of riding. Both Walter Ohman and Glen Cain recall clearly that they lost the trail soon after leaving Addis Ababa. In Marako they spent one day of prayer for guidance and then continued to the south. An insightful Ethiopian stated, "It was God's plan that the party's direction to Jimma was to be confused, because God's thinking is different from that of human beings."

To add flavor to the journey and to show how the gospel was first explained to my ancestors I am including the following two journal entries of Clarence Duff, a missionary in that first party.

FIRST ENTRY

March 19, 1928

Part of my work in camp is to see that feed for the mules and horses is provided regularly. As it is so near the end of the dry season there is almost no grass to be cut, so that we have to buy hay or barley or whatever we can find. I often go out with some of our men to look for feed, and frequently have some very interesting conversations with the native people in the course of our buying. Gamatchu, who interprets quite well, asked me to go with him to look at some barley he had found. The people were nearly all in their houses. We were invited into one of them. The house was a typical round hut. The walls are made of poles plastered with mud. The roof is upheld by a center pole from which about halfway up from the ground eight or nine brace-poles branch out to halfway points. There are no windows and but one door, to enter which required that one stoop a little. As I entered, several people rose from the fire near the center of the hut and offered me the best seat, on a rug that covered a slightly raised place in the dirt floor close to the smoky little fire.

One of the men offered me a big pipe made from a gourd with a long stem reaching from the floor to one's mouth. When I declined this they brought me a wooden platter with some freshly-parched Indian corn. It was really very good, and furnished an opening topic of conversation as I munched, asking what they called it, and praised its fine qualities as a food.

The house was 15 feet in diameter. Behind rough pole stanchions along the far side of the room stood six cows peacefully chewing their cud. Just back of me were the same number of sheep. These animals must all be brought into the house at night to keep them safe from thieves and hyenas. What space was left was occupied by the family, father and mother and four children. While I was there, of course, there were as many visitors as could get inside the door.

One of the women in a jocular mood said she wanted to sell me her boy, a little fellow of about six years of age without a stitch of clothes on him for a time (a silver coin worth about 3 and a half cents). I told her I knew she loved her little boy, but she insisted that she didn't like him, and wanted me to take him for a servant or a slave. I almost was beginning to believe she was in earnest, when suddenly she admitted that she was joking; then she said, "Bless my child." She was really serious about this, but I told her I could not do that; only God could bless. I said though, that I would be glad to pray to God and ask Him to bless her child and all of them.

Then I asked if they had heard about the little Christ-child who came from God's throne and they said they hadn't. I told them about him, how he was born among the cattle and sheep, perhaps very much as their own children were born, how he became a man and did such kind things to everyone in need, how he died such a cruel death for our sakes so that we might not have to pay the price of our sin, how he went back to his Father's house but promised to come again as he had gone. They all listened very eagerly and then bowed their heads reverently while I asked God to bless them and teach them to love his Son.

While I was there the man in the next house had offered to sell me the milk from one cow for a timun, and now he urged me to come into his house to see the cow milked. I sent Gamatchu for one of our vessels, but before he returned the man had begun to milk into his own little gourd. The calf always has to have its turn first, else the cow refuses to give any milk at all. It is hard for me to believe that these cows cannot be trained to give milk without such indulgence, but those who have been in Africa for many years insist that it cannot be done.

While Gamatchu was away I carried on an interesting, if not so amusing, conversation using all the Amharic words I knew and asking the names for various articles and animals. This house was even more crowded than the other for there were eight cows, six or seven sheep, and a roost full of chickens just above the door. The cow gave less than a quart of milk and half of that, the boy said, was water that had been in the gourd since morning. Our men refused to take the milk, saying it would not be fit to use at all when boiled; but I told them I would keep my bargain, for I was much more interested in getting an entrance into the house than I was in buying milk.

These people had many questions to ask. They wanted to know from what country I came. I told them I came from America and had traveled on a ship for almost six weeks to get there. They were amazed at that and asked why I should come so far away from home. I told them then about One who had come much further than that for their sakes and mine, One who had left far more than I had left behind; and they listened intently while I told them as simply as I could the story of Jesus and his love.

They said, as so many others have said to me as I have talked with them along the way: "What you tell us is very good. We have never heard it before." They said they would keep what I had told them in their hearts, and they thanked me as I went out. I bought my barley and went back to the tent praying that God might honor the simple faith of these people, and that though we had to go on at sunrise the next morning, he might send someone to teach them more about him.

SECOND ENTRY

February 26, 1930

This has been written in installments. After I had written about half of it, some six or eight men came to sit down outside the tent door. They watched for a while, then they said: "We old men have come. Aren't you going to talk to us? What talk have you brought? Do you have medicine? Why have you come to this place? Aren't you going to tell us God's words?" So I sat on a box in front of the tent and talked to them quite a long time. I said I had no medicine, only one kind. I had heart medicine. Every man's heart is sick. Sin has spoiled it. I said I had God's Book here, and God said there that every man is dying. Every man that does not know God and Jesus Christ, his Son, is just like a dead man. But God wants to give him life so he sent his only Son to be man's guarantor, or substitute. When we believe on him, God gives us life. Jesus is the medicine for sick hearts. Jesus Christ came to save sinners. Away across the hill in Sankure, where we were this morning, men told me that Mohammed did not save sinners, he saved good men. But that does not help you and me any. If only good men are to be saved, then you and I cannot be saved, for I am a sinner and you are sinners. We need a sinner-saving man. Where can you find a without-sin man? Some men say they are good, or that other men are good, but God doesn't say that. He says all men are bad. Every man's heart is evil and every man does bad works. God loves sinning men, but he cannot stand sin. God's only Son, died for them. His blood ran out. And now, when we believe in him he washes our hearts with that blood, and destroys all the sin. God gives us a new heart. But Jesus Christ didn't come to save good men, he came to save sinners. Why have we come here? Just to tell you this. We don't have anything to take from your country. We have fathers and mothers and brothers and sisters and many friends in our own country. If we wanted land and cows and sheep, we could have all we wanted there. We don't have any "selling things," we just have free-giving" things. God doesn't sell anything. He only gives. You can't buy life from God. He gives everlasting life to you when you believe Jesus.

And with many interruptions and many explanations and much repetition I try to satisfy their curiosity and quiet their apprehensions, destroy all grounds for their suspicion, and reduce the Good News to its simplest terms. (End of Duff journal entries.)

Now, please return with me to that first spirit-directed journey to my ancestors. You see I am a member of the Kambatta tribe of south-central Ethiopia.

As the Lambie party neared Hosanna, the capital of Kambatta and their neighboring tribe Hadiya, they were met by the chief of Kambatta. With him was a welcoming committee--a great crowd of warriors and civilian people who escorted them to the governor's residence. There Dr. Lambie was astonished to find Dejazmatch Meshesha, a former patient from his days in Wollega. The Dejazmatch was the godfather of Ras Teferi who had become Emperor Haile Selassie! He was also governor of that region.

Governor Meshesha informed Dr. Lambie that others of his former patients from his days in Wollega were governors in the neighboring regions of Wolayitta (Wo-lay-ta) and Sidama!

The Lambie party ceased to be concerned about reaching their original goal, Jimma. They now understood that God had directed their steps to these former Lambie patients who had become leaders of their people! Because of them, the missionaries were given freedom to preach the gospel, and one by one the people began to respond.

The first and second baptisms took place in Sidama in December, 1932, the third baptism took place in Wolayitta in December, 1933. The fourth baptism took place in Kambatta and Hadiya in April, 1934. These four people groups, Sidama, Wolayitta, Kambatta and Hadiya became the most responsive to the gospel message.

By God's grace on February 16, 1933, Dr. Lambie, Clarence Duff and John Phillips set out from Soddu to search for a site that would be a satisfactory place to start the work among my people group. Soddu is the main town among the Wolayitta tribe and place where the Lambie party had settled. On that day in February Clarence Duff and John Phillips pitched their tents at Tezza, an area about three miles outside the town of Durame.

In 1934, Dr. Bingham, founder of the mission known at that time as Sudan Interior Mission, visited the Tezza mission station on his way back to Addis Ababa from the Wolayitta conference during his visit to Ethiopia in 1934. He found that Mr. Phillips had built three small huts on the eastern side of Ambaricho Mountain. These huts were for medical treatment, to teach the English and Amharic alphabets, and to preach the gospel.

The missionaries provided job opportunities for some of the needy people in the area, medical treatment for those who came to the station for medical assistance, and food and clothes for those who were in desperate need (orphans and widows). Such a holistic approach to the gospel message created a positive attitude in the society and gradual acceptance of the gospel among the Kambatta people.

But Satan was not about to give up his territory without a fight. In 1934, the missionaries began to face many challenges. There was opposition from witchdoctors, Ethiopian Orthodox Church leaders and landlords. Those early missionaries also faced the tremendous challenges of shortage of food and water during their itinerant evangelistic activities while walking to the different villages of Kambatta. Be-that-as-it-may, they boldly preached the gospel in the market places. This led to some entering the Kingdom of God.

In addition to the challenges of the work on the local level, there were the disturbing events of World War II. Following the defeat of the Ethiopian government troops on March 31, 1936 by Mussolini of Italy, Emperor Haile Selassie left for England to seek help from the League of Nations. Three days later on May 5, 1936, Addis Ababa came under the control of the Italian authorities. The news spread all over the country and looting and violence began on a wide scale. On June 28th, 1936, Mr. Phillips received news that the Tezza

Mission station had been ransacked. He was not able to go back because of the spirit of anarchy that ran rampant throughout the country. He wandered from house to house and village to village, hiding from the rebels. Finally, he headed to Wolayitta to join other SIM missionaries. On April 17, 1937, they departed to Addis Ababa on the way to their home countries.

The Italian colonizers gave promise of freedom, but shortly those few evangelical Christians in southern Ethiopia, especially in Wolayitta, Kambatta and Hadiya, began to face severe persecution by the Italian authorities. The Italians linked these Ethiopian believers to: 1) Their international enemies of that day - the United States and Great Britain; 2) Since the new evangelical converts were very active in reading and writing Amharic, the national language of Ethiopia, in order to read and preach the Bible, and the fact that the goal of the Italian authorities was to change the Amharic script into the Latin script, the Amharic language seemed to them like a great threat to Italian control in that region; 3) They imagined that the evangelicals were creating a negative outlook against fascism all over the country; 4) The Christians prayed for peace and security for their country, and for their king, Haile Selassie, who was exiled in Great Britain. This fact was hated by the Italians who thought that Christians were cunningly praying for the downfall of fascism in Ethiopia. Therefore, such things prompted the fascists to watch the new believers carefully and to try to extinguish their faith in Christ through harsh treatment.

However, during those days everybody was a preacher to everybody, at home, in the market place, at funerals and in their family get-togethers. The consecrated and transformed lives of believers were also an incredibly powerful witness to the unbelievers drawing them to the light of the gospel.

Raymond Davis recalls how the church in southern Ethiopia began to move forward. He was one of the SIM missionaries who was forced to leave southern Ethiopia because of the Italian occupation. He wrote the following after he saw the incredible growth of the Church following his return after 5 years absence.

Before we left them (the new believers) we had increasingly emphasized their responsibility to reach their own people with the gospel, and they were already speaking boldly about Jesus Christ. They were also meeting together on their own for prayer and church services. "We are leaving you, but God will not leave you" had been our parting words to them. The first three months on their own, was a time of testing and self-examination with a great deal of prayer. Then the persecution came, but as thirsty cattle turn to refreshing water, so the people began to turn to God. People began to leave their satanic worship and pagan practices. The tiny churches began to send out preachers two by two, baptizing those who believed. Soon even the unbelievers were eager to hear the Word of God. As many hundreds turned to God, branch churches were established. By the second year it was necessary to build church buildings and choose local leaders. Looking back on these days, one can see the strategy of the Holy Spirit for the Church. He raised up strong courageous individuals through whom He eventually caused the gospel to move like *wild fire* throughout the land.

Evangelist Alemu Himbaro also writes how the first converts of Kambatta and Hadiya impacted the society through their Christian faith, and how the Lord enabled the church to be sustained through the difficult period of the Italian occupation:

The new Christian believers were very committed and serious about putting the words of the Bible into practice as part of their daily life. They were helping the poor and sharing with them whatever they had; supporting the widows, orphans and the persecuted believers; building houses for the needy and churches in a single day; bringing food for Christian brothers in prison on a daily basis and cultivating their land in order to support their family members who were in prison for preaching. They demonstrated their lived-out Christian faith to the other community members with amazing love and unity. Such amazing practical and crystal-clear Christian life practices really frustrated and weakened the persecutors and eventually brought about the extinction of the witchdoctors and animism in the region. Also, Christians began to live and model the life of hard workers in the society. Their spiritual and social transformation had a tremendous impact on the society such as dressing with clean clothes, introducing new crops such as potatoes, sugar cane, bananas, oranges and coffee plantations for their living and as cash crops and to support their children in school. Such things brought a tremendous positive impact on the whole society which resulted today in the conversion of the majority of the Kambatta and Hadiya people to the Christian faith.

So, the missionaries' absence was replaced by the presence, intervention, and power of the Holy Spirit among the new believers. The Spirit of God was doing through all of them the work of witnessing, empowering, and illuminating the Word. He was giving them boldness and fueling these preachers of the Gospel for the expansion of God's Kingdom in the Kambatta, Hadiya, and Wolayitta regions.

After the eviction of the Italians, persecution was intensified by the nationals. The following history was what some of the first believers told me:

"When the white people (missionaries) arrived, they began to tell us about the good news of Jesus Christ which was real good news for the Kambatta people who were living under physical and spiritual bondage. But both landlords and witchdoctors became furious and began to persecute the missionaries and the new believers. They were afraid that all the people would be liberated from their dominion. Therefore, intense persecution spread like wildfire in all directions; witchdoctors, government officials and landlords raised mobs against the new believers.

But God by His grace and mercy gave them perseverance, boldness, faith and courage in the midst of imprisonments and beatings. God enabled the believers to stand strong in their faith even unto death. Two of the first Christians, Fitamo and Boke, died because of unbearable beatings in prison by the government police. Fuenuro, Mantamo, Hosisso, and Ba'e passed away in prison because of the suffering of many years of imprisonment. But Christianity continued to grow. Christians became stronger, churches continued to multiply and young Christians became educated."

Today, everything has completely changed! Most of the persecutors have become Christians. Currently, there is no witchdoctor worship among the Kambatta people group. God also changed the political leadership so that the children of the persecuted Christians became political leaders, professors, doctors, office managers, engineers, pastors, evangelists and missionaries. Of the total current Kambatta population of 800,000 more than 94% are evangelical Christians. We now have many big churches in the towns of Kambatta gathering by the thousands for Sunday worship services. Also conferences are conducted with modern sound systems and different technical equipment. Almost all the churches have caught the vision of sending missionaries to the unreached people groups of Ethiopia and beyond. Already more than 200 cross-cultural missionaries have been sent out among the unreached people groups of Ethiopia and more than 10 missionaries have been sent out as cross-cultural missionaries outside Ethiopia.

We rejoice to see the amazing growth of the churches everywhere among the Kambatta people. This is the outcome of the huge sacrifice paid by our Christian forefathers and pioneer missionaries. Therefore, we owe a huge debt to them and we must not forget about the suffering of the first believers, our spiritual forefathers. However, this is not the end of this wonderful story. It is only the beginning!

Clarence Duff and his wife.

Dr. Lambie and his wife Charlotte

The first team of SIM missionaries to Ethiopia.
Top left to right, Mr. Glen Cain, Dr. Lambie, Mr. Earl Lewis, Betty Lambie, Mr. Rasmussen, Mr. Clarence Duff, Mr. George Rhoad. Seated, Mrs. Lambie, Mrs. Rasmussen, George Rhoad Jr., Mrs. Rhoad

Chapter Five

The Church Matures

By God's providence I was blessed to get my doctorate at Western Seminary in Portland, Oregon. That happened between 2006-2009. As part of my thesis I wrote a history of the Kambatta church. It tells how the church matured. Three documents were sent to me by the families of Ralph Jacobson and Gus Kayser. What I share in this chapter is taken from these documents. Though I was not taught by these two men, most of those who taught me were taught by them.

Ralph Jacobson and Gus Kayser were used by God to build a strong foundation for the Kambatta church. It was based on the teaching of the Word of God. Mr. Jacobson, riding his mule, Alganesh ("she is my bed"), taught God's Word to the Kambatta church leaders who, because of family responsibilities and other reasons, could not attend the resident Bible school on the mission compound. Gus Kayser ran the Bible school on the mission compound and prepared the notes used by both men. During those years, 1950's and 60's, the mimeograph machine was never idle on the Tezza Mission Station. These two men, gifted and empowered by God's Spirit, wove God's Word deeply into the fabric of the Kambatta people. The Lord mightily moved in Kambatta from 1952 -1965 as recalled by Ralph and Doris Jacobson and Lois Kayser. By the time I was writing my thesis Gus Kayser was in heaven. I will allow the Jacobsons and Lois Kayser to tell their stories.

THE JACOBSON AND LOIS KAYSER ACCOUNTS

July 27, 1952 was a cold, wet, foggy morning. Charlie Bonk had brought us from Sheshemane to Durame, Tezza, a distance of about 50 miles. During the night we had traveled through the Arussi Desert winding around huge mud holes left by heavy Italian trucks.

Crossing the Belatey River was a harrowing experience, as we crawled over the rocks of Cry In Vain Valley as it was called. Charlie, with Dick Spahr's help, had prepared a temporary dwelling for us and had also put up the frame of our house. Now they were eager to leave before the heavy rains made the already difficult trail impassable. Quickly unloading our boxes, our friends left.

Alone, with our nine-month old baby girl, Abebech, we were thankful for a bed, for a stove and a roof over our heads. Admittedly, the dirt floor and the wet mud walls were a new experience.

Following the Italian occupation, my wife, Doris and I had the privilege of being the first resident missionaries at Tezza, Durame, remaining there from July 1952 to July 1965. Initially there were no clinics, no schools, no roads, no telephone, and no electricity. Few Kambattans spoke Amharic, the national language of Ethiopia. Bibles were scarce and we knew no one.

How thrilling it was, then, to meet pockets of believers who were so friendly and so eager to learn more of God's Word. During the Italian occupation many had become believers but had little teaching . As they came to welcome us, we soon learned that we were among special friends. As we became better acquainted, it became evident that we shared similar characteristics: strong-willed, persistent and hard working. A special surprise was when Ato Shequte, an older church leader, accompanied by two others, stopped by to welcome us as they journeyed by mule the 50 miles from Soddu to Hosanna. Later, Mr. and Mrs. Couser, also traveling by mule from Soddu, came to greet us. These visits were a great encouragement in our early days in Kambatta.

In God's plan we had arrived at a critical time. An epidemic was causing many deaths. We learned that in a neighboring hut three people had died the night before we arrived. Thankfully I had received one year of basic medical training in New York and the Lord allowed me to help many sick people at that time using the newly available treatments of penicillin injections and sulfa drugs. These proved to be very effective and, by God's grace, many lives were spared. To my knowledge all who received treatment recovered. The results brought glory to God and much good will among the people.

Satan worship was an even greater problem than the epidemic. Witch doctors exerted great power and demonic forces abounded. We realized that we, with these believers, were about to engage in very real spiritual warfare in which we all would need to "put on the whole armor of God" with heavy doses of God's Word and prayer. In Kambatta, the witch doctor ruled the lives of many. For example, when the uncle of one of our workers was very sick, he sacrificed virtually all his herd to appease the spirits, but to no avail. This story was typical.

New believers, wanting to express the transformation in their lives, drew from their experiences of suddenly meeting Italian soldiers during the occupation. Immediately dropping whatever was in their hands, they would raise both arms high as a sign of surrender. When they learned that Jesus was more powerful than Satan, they chose to acknowledge Jesus as their new Master in the same way. Raising both hands they would say, "I renounce Satan; I accept Jesus Christ as my Lord and Savior"! (To this day that is how you become a Christian in Kambatta).

I believe the main key to church growth in Kambatta was this 'turn-about-face'. Many told me that after receiving the Lord Jesus as their personal Savior, their lives were so transformed that when they would meet former acquaintances on the trail, people would stop and ask them, "Why are you so different?" They would answer that they no longer feared Satan and the evil spirits because Jesus had overcome Satan. As they shared this Good News many believed.

Believers shared the Gospel wherever they went. One special lady used to bring food each week to her son and daughter at school. It was a long journey taking four or five hours by foot. Each trip she made a habit of stopping at different homes and asking for a drink of water. Sitting down, she would then share the story of 'living water' with her host.

In Geyota (district), Ato Awano led Ato Abide to the Lord, and Ato Abide led Ato Abuye and Ato Samuel to the Lord. It was the wonderful story of people telling people telling people. (Coming to Tezza some years later, David Mai found Ato Abide was the clinic evangelist, Ato Abuye was the Bible School director, and Ato Samuel was the clinic head dresser. A dresser is a combination nurse and physician's assistant. These men were a delight to work with).

God demonstrated His power by the transformation of Ato Bamborey from slave trader to soul winner. This was reminiscent of the 18th century story of converted slave trader John Newton. Because of Ato Bamborey's changed life many people turned from being slaves of Satan to servants of God.

However, there was strong opposition. After making a profession of salvation, believers told me how, during the night, chunks of dried mud would be hurled at them as they tried to sleep in their homes. Demons are real. Fellow believers would join them in prayer and would overcome the evil one in Jesus' powerful name. The chunks of flying mud ceased!

One morning a crowd of men, all carrying long spears, stopped at our little, two-room mud house. They were on their way up Ambaricho mountain to ask the witch doctor to pray for rain. Later I learned that the witch doctor had put rancid butter on his head, crawled into a cave and the poisonous snakes licked the butter off - a sign, he said, that their prayer had been heard. But there was still no rain. Following the example of Elijah in the Bible, the believers prayed and God answered with rain. There was great rejoicing!

As a teenager, Ato Boltano was very ill for several months. Nothing seemed to help. Late one night his father came to our door urgently pleading for help. I was in Addis Ababa so my wife, Doris, asked Mr. Kayser and Mr. Campbell to go. They went but could not determine the cause of his sickness so they fervently prayed for his healing. God graciously answered prayer and in the morning Boltano came to our compound, well and thankful.

During a seven year period, 1952-1959, there was much persecution. Initially, I had been invited to speak at the different churches. It was a joy. But then I learned that the authorities would come the next day to take those who had gathered and imprison them. I wanted to stop these visits. But the people said, "We don't mind, why should you?" Hardly a week went by without at least a handful, and sometimes several dozen, believers being put in the local prison. While there they were beaten with hippo hide whips.

The prison guards loved it when believers were thrown in prison. It meant the guards would have plenty of good food as they would eat what they wanted from the supply Christians provided for their fellow believers who were in prison . However, the officials and religious leaders were very angry because they could not stop this great movement from spreading! One governor angrily shouted, "I put you in prison because you were preaching. Now, in prison you are still preaching! What can I do with you?!"

Ethiopian Orthodox Church priests had encouraged government authorities to imprison many believers. Allegations included meeting without permission and being enemies of Mary. At one point, 70 men were forced to march barefoot and without food across the Arussi Desert all the way to Assela, where they were imprisoned. It was an 80 mile trip! Marching in the heat of the day they crossed dried river beds and dug with bare hands in the sand to get water. Through swollen lips they sipped the moisture from the sand.

They were held for six months. In prison the men continued to share the good news with fellow prisoners and guards. Many who heard, believed. Two believers died in prison, Ato Futnoro and, I think, Ato Muntamo, Halango's brother. Ato Fochei died after being released. Ato Leggessa Segaro was held in prison for two years. There was great rejoicing when he came home. During this time of intense persecution, the churches flourished and the believers went everywhere preaching the gospel. Their homes were burned and cattle were stolen but through it all the amazing response was "the more we suffered, the more we loved our Savior, and the faster the church grew."

Everywhere people were telling people the Good News that through Jesus' death, God offered them forgiveness of sin; and because Jesus rose from the dead we too have hope of eternal life. Jesus had overcome Satan's greatest power, the power of death.

In large gatherings and in homes people would share this Good News. Christian funerals played a significant role in the spread of the Gospel. Great crowds would gather. Instead of wailing and hopelessness, there was peace and singing. Usually, four elders would stand together and as they sensed the Lord's leading, they would take turns sharing the good news of the hope Christians have. Everyone at the funeral heard the Gospel and many accepted the Lord as their Savior.

Another occasion for large gatherings was when people publicly shared their testimony through baptism. Rivulets of people coming from all directions converged on the baptismal site. Baptism was a symbol of "no turning back". It was also the point at which persecution intensified. But persecution did not dampen the peoples' request for this sacrament. When the Mai family came on the scene it was not uncommon to have 8000 people witness the baptism of 400 to 500 at a time. Newly baptized believers would participate together in the Lord's Table.

In wedding ceremonies Christian couples would hold the Bible between them. This became symbolic of the happy couple's oneness in Christ.

Because people were so radically and dramatically transformed by the good news which proclaimed freedom for those enslaved by Satan, the Church grew rapidly. This, in my view, was the primary factor behind the tremendous church growth: the radical transformation wrought by the mighty power of the Holy Spirit in individual lives, resulting in believers sharing their new-found faith with everyone they met.

I believe a second factor in the rapid growth of the Church was the Holy Spirit's guidance in the spread of small churches, as opposed to larger, centralized congregations. This created an urgent need for the leadership in each church, usually four elders, to become well- grounded in God's Word.

As we discussed with the elders the rapidly growing need for more leaders, it was agreed that we should start a special class for elders, meeting at Tezza every Tuesday from 10 in the morning until 3 in the afternoon. We allowed time for the elders to discuss church issues among themselves. Between 60 and 80 men would come from the three closest districts: Ambursi, Geyota, and Kacha.

We studied basic teachings of the gospel, church growth in Acts, and later went on to study the great doctrines of the church in the Epistles. Recently, as I (Ralph Jacobson) reread a letter that I had written in January 1954, I was reminded that in our study in the Book of Romans, the first verse alone took considerable time as we discussed the attitude of a spiritual worker compared to that of a carnal worker. More detailed studies, however, only became possible through the Bible School program which was begun shortly thereafter.

Young men were eager to study God's Word, as well. With the elders' approval, it was agreed that Bible Study classes for these younger men would be held every Friday and well over one hundred came regularly to my classes.
The Mishgida* elders appointed Shamebo to be my co-worker, guide and interpreter. He was a "God-send" and served us faithfully and effectively.

God gave much wisdom to the leaders who, as the churches multiplied, organized groups of churches into districts called **sebats under the umbrella of the Wengelawit (Fellowship of Kambatta churches). Elders from each church would meet together in a sebat as often as every two weeks; then leading elders from each sebat would meet once a month. The Lord blessed this method of dealing with Church 'growing pains', as the leaders met regularly and came to agreement on church policy and practices.

There was a great spirit of unity among Church elders as we studied God's Word and the elders would discuss among themselves concerns and problems. They told me that any time I could show from Scripture that what they were doing was wrong - or what they should do - there would be no argument. God's Word was the final court of appeal!

There were several difficult issues that the elders dealt with over time. For example, the matter of alcohol. The elders came to the conclusion that it was not appropriate to imbibe alcoholic drinks and reasoned that they had seen how it had hindered the Lord's work. A couple of examples were cited: Traveling to Elders' meetings they would become thirsty. Women sitting under the shade of a tree would sell tej or tella, local alcoholic drinks. The men would stop to rest and have a drink. The result, they said, was that in the meeting some would become drowsy, others argumentative. At a wedding feast two men got into an argument and in a drunken rage, one bit off the other's finger. The elders chose not to continue using intoxicating drink. It wasn't long before they felt God had provided a substitute, a honey drink that one of the elders from Beynara developed! It was called 'honey water.'

*Mishgida was the name of one of the original districts of the Kambatta Church. **Sebat is the Amharic word for seven. Originally, there were seven districts that made up the Kambatta Church. The name for district, Sebat, was kept even though the church grew and was divided into more than seven districts.

.

Another problem that was dealt with in a similar fashion was the use and sale of tobacco. One of the elders shared his experience. He had planted tobacco in a place behind the inset (false banana) patch where it would not be seen. When he harvested it, he tied it in bundles and put it on a shelf in his home covering it with animal skins. But his conscience bothered him and he wanted to get rid of it once and for all. However, he couldn't sell it locally where he was known, so getting up early one morning he loaded the tobacco on his donkey and set out to sell the tobacco. Coming to an elderly woman sitting on the ground, he decided to offer her a bargain price just to get rid of it. But the woman, squinting up in the bright sunlight, began typical bargaining. After some time he exclaimed,

"A Christian has only one price!" Her response, "A Christian doesn't sell tobacco." This lesson became a guidepost for many.

Yet another major decision had to do with marriage and multiple wives. At the time it was not uncommon to have several wives. As the elders studied God's Word, they became convinced that, clearly under the New Covenant, it was God's plan that each man should have his own wife, accepting that the first wife was the legitimate spouse. Then the concern was what should they do with the other wives? They told me that they had long discussions and much prayer and in the end, the elders concluded that they should live with only one, the first one, but they were to be responsible for providing housing and care for the others until God provided husbands for them. In most cases the women had accepted the Lord as their personal Savior along with the men. They, too, wanted to be free from living in sin. At that time medical help was scarce. Many women died in child-birth. Their bereaved husbands would be looking for a good Christian wife to care for them and their families, so in time God provided husbands for all these women.

In granting approval for opening new stations, the Emperor, Haile Selassie, had insisted that an immediate priority was to begin elementary schooling. So, before I could complete our house, we built a tukul (mud hut with grass roof) by the little river. There I taught a dozen eager students for two hours a day. I have heard that from that simple beginning, two of the initial students went on to obtain their doctorates. Under John Campbell's leadership within four years the school rapidly expanded to 450 students.

A major step forward was taken when the elders expressed some concern that there was a growing rift between these elementary students--with their education and ability to read--and the church. After much prayer and discussion it was agreed that after grade 4, each student would be required to teach literacy in the local churches for one year before going on to grade 5. The elders felt this was God's provision for healing that rift. In the process over a period of some 5 or 6 years it was estimated that as many as 18,000 people had learned to read and write at these local Church schools. Another multiplier effect!

Because there was a great desire to be better prepared to serve the Lord, the elders were anxious to start a proper Bible School. There was another problem that needed to be addressed. We had heard stories of some evangelists who had taken their wives to distant places. The food was different. The language was different. It was hard for the women and they became homesick. As we discussed this problem with the elders, I pointed out that the women had not received the same training as the men. They did not have the same vision; they could not share the same burden. I shared that Doris and I had attended the same Bible School, had received the same training and had shared the same burden. The Kambatta women needed this, too. We encouraged the elders to consider a Married Couples Bible School. After several months of prayer it was agreed that the churches would build housing for the married students, the students would provide their own food, and we would provide the classrooms and instruction. When the community saw hundreds of men bringing materials and doing the work freely, they were amazed! "Why would all these people brings loads of bamboo, split wood, and bundles of grass and do all this work and not get paid?" In all, 49 huts were built by some 2500 people. Later these were upgraded to tin-roofed buildings.

The Kaysers, who served in a place called Goba, had started a successful Bible School as soon as they had a few believers. The Mission leaders felt that the Kaysers were ideal for the important job of establishing a Bible School at Tezza.. Gus and Lois Kayser were re-assigned to work among the Kambattans in 1955. Gus built the Bible School building and became the Principal.

LOIS KAYSER'S ACCOUNT

When we opened the Bible School in Durame, the men were taught by Gus and the women were taught by Doris Jacobsen, Hope Russel, the resident nurse, and me. The women were not educated nor did they know Amharic so they could not keep up with the men, who would be studying deeply into the Bible. The women had Bible class and were taught to read and write Amharic. They were also taught things that would help them in their homes--things that they could teach other women wherever their ministry would lead them, such as basic hygiene, child care, sewing and knitting.

There was very little Bible school material available when Gus started to teach. He bought a mimeograph machine so that he could copy his lesson material in the form of questions that the students could study every night in preparation for the next day's class. Ato Leggessa Segaro, the man who survived a lengthy imprisonment in Assela, was helping with the Commentaries on each of the Books of the Bible making sure that the Amharic was correct. I copied on stencils all of the Commentaries that Gus wrote. Every Saturday Gus put the stencils on the mimeograph machine and made many copies. Ato Shemabo put the copies together to form books. We did this for eleven years until the mission began to print for us.

JACOBSON ACCOUNT CONCLUSION

It was a thrill to learn that this Bible School continued to function throughout the Communist era and on to this very day. In addition, the first District Bible School, established by the church, was led by Ato Asajz. I am convinced that the multiplication of District Bible Schools became another major factor for solid church growth.

Just as the school program resulted in expanded literacy, and as the Bible School program multiplied Bible Schools, so, too, from Soddu Dr. Barlow's medical training of dressers multiplied health clinics around the Kambatta countryside.

The yearly conference was a time of great joy and spontaneous giving reminiscent of the Macedonian believers who gave "out of the most severe trial, their overflowing joy and extreme poverty welled up in rich generosity - giving even beyond their ability" (2 Cor. 8:2-3). At the annual conference, with thousands of people gathered together worshipping God, evangelists returning home shared what God was doing. With leading elders exhorting the people, I witnessed "hilarious" giving (2 Cor 9:7) and much rejoicing along with young people dedicating their lives to the Lord's work.

Another amazing gift of God was that of antiphonal singing. The leader would chant or sing a Bible truth and the congregation would repeat the same truth. This powerful teaching tool instructing pre-literate people had a great multiplier effect. Great truths of Scripture were implanted in the hearts and minds of those who participated.

Another personal highlight was when I was able to return, in small measure, the hospitality I had so often received from different churches by inviting elders to join me for a three-week Wengelawit Elders' Rainy Season Bible Study Course. Mr. Kayser shared with me in leading the classes, and my wife Doris provided fresh bread each day which proved to be a big 'hit'. A photo I have shows more than 40 leading elders from Kambatta and Hadiya present at one of these courses. It was a time of mutual encouragement and fellowship. I recall a comment made by Ato Shegute in our last gathering. In a speech of appreciation, he said, "Others have come offering us many things; you offered us only one thing, the Word of God, and we want to thank you."

MANY YEARS LATER

One of my greatest thrills was to return to Durame many years later for a visit. Early Sunday morning, my former colleague Ato Shamebo and I walked down to Zato and, as we approached Aba (daddy of) Asafa's place unannounced, we saw a packed church of young people studying God's Word, led by Ato Mekore.

The Church grew and through persecution was purified. The Church grew because "God so loved the world that He gave His only Son" who willingly gave His life to redeem sinful men. The Church grew because redeemed sinners were transformed and empowered by the Holy Spirit to fulfill our Savior's last command to "Go and Tell". Our first Bible School Class Motto was "As the Father hath sent Me, even so send I you". God's church in Kambatta remains committed to that Great Commission and today is going into all the world with the Gospel.

Mr. and Mrs. Ralph Jacobson with their
first child.

Annual Mission Conference to
mobilize believers for Missions

The annual Mission Conference also
mobilized many believers to serve on
the mission field.

Leaders of the church who God mightily used to mature the Kambatta church

Ralph and
Doris Jacobson
with their
growing
Children at
Durame Teze
compound.

Perilous travel
for the pioneer
missionaries
trying to reach
their Durame
Teza compound

Bible school teaching staff. (left to right, Tareqegn Adebo, Shamebo Mekiso, Gustav Kayser and Legesse Segaro)

The first Bible school at the Durame Teza compound. The students lived in the grass roof huts.

Ralph Jacobson and Gustav Kayser with the Bible school graduates.

Chapter Six

Early Schooling

God has always prepared His servants for the job He wants them to do. He prepared Moses by giving him forty years in Pharaoh's court where he was schooled in all the learning of Egypt. There followed forty years of survival training on the back side of the Midian Desert. Paul, whom Jesus described as "My chosen instrument" left home in Tarsus for education. He traveled to Jerusalem to be taught by the best, Gamaliel, a religious expert and very popular teacher. As I look back on my schooling, I can see God's provision for me, too!

I begin this important part of my preparation by sharing with you the life story of SIM missionary John Campbell. God used Mr. Campbell to introduce my people to the idea of universal education-education for everyone not just a few privileged people.

JOHN CAMPBELL STORY

John Edward Campbell arrived on December 13,1928, the second child of dairy and beef farmers Harvey and Grace Campbell. They were living in the small community of Stalwart, located in the Upper Peninsula of Michigan. The family soon moved to Pickford, Michigan where John grew up. They struggled through the depression years and for a while John's uncle and his family lived with them. John always worked on the farm with his dad and older brother but when his brother was drafted into WWII, John's responsibilities increased. His father was not well and sometimes only three days of school a week were managed.

1946 was a good year for John. He graduated from high school and his brother returned from the war. For two years the three men worked together, and the farm was prospering; but John began to hear the Lord calling him to a different vocation.

His spiritual journey started when he was 4 years old and although the family rarely went to church, his father was concerned that John hadn't been baptized. Dad took young John to the parsonage and the minister baptized him. A little later, while his dad was working in the woods tapping maple trees, he saw a vision of Christ on the cross. He threw his cigarettes on the ground and from then on the family faithfully attended church. John accepted Christ as his Savior when he was 11 years old and during his teen years committed himself fully to the Lord.

John talked to his pastor about where to go, to prepare for full-time service. The pastor pointed John to his alma mater, Bob Jones University. John entered Bob Jones in the fall of '48 and had only been there a short while when SIM missionary Carl Tanus spoke in chapel and John felt God's call to Africa. During his college years, he was active in the Mission Prayer Band, the college radio program 'Missions on the March' and in services held in churches, missions, jails, pool halls and on the street.

John graduated in 1952 and applied to Sudan Interior Mission. In July 1954 he sailed from New York for Africa, arriving the next month in Ethiopia to begin language school. But upon arriving, he was told that he was needed in Sheshemane Leprosarium to build much needed housing for the leprosy patients. When that phase of the building was completed, he headed to Debre Birhan to begin language school. He was there just three weeks when he was again assigned to a building project, this time at

Kallafo because the builder was due for furlough. That brief stay in language school was important. During that time John met another language student, a missionary nurse, Marje Hawes.

Kallafo, though in Ethiopia, was mainly populated by Somali Muslims. John had brought some soccer balls with him and started inviting the workers to play soccer with him after work. It wasn't long before there were about 100 youth coming with 4 games going on simultaneously each afternoon. John invited them to come back on Sunday, his holy day, and he would give a short message. Most of them came but when he asked them to invite their parents, they laughed telling him that if their parents realized they were attending a Bible study none would be allowed to return. John and his message were not appreciated as is brought out in the following story:

John was the only missionary at the station since the medical staff all had to leave because of a pending court case. He slept outside due to the heat and one night the local leaders decided to murder John. When his cook came to work the next morning, he asked John. "Who was it that was guarding you last night?" John didn't know about any guards so the cook explained that when the town's people had arrived at the compound, they found John surrounded by soldiers so they returned to their homes knowing they could not carry out their plans "The angel of the Lord encamps around those who fear Him and rescues them." Psalm 34:7.

After the buildings were completed, John was again assigned to language school and while there, Marge Hawes whom he had met previously, arrived to be the hostess. Marje loved her nursing and was not one bit happy to leave it to become hostess. But God had plans to get her married whether she liked it or not. Romance soon blossomed. They were engaged in February and per SIM policy, John was assigned to Durame to take over the school and Marje to the Soddu Hospital. They were married at Bishoftu, the mission vacation compound, on July 6, 1957.

John continued to oversee the academic school at Durame-Tezza and Marje the clinic. He came up with a plan that after the students finished their 4th year, they return to their home areas to teach children and adults in their churches reading and writing for a year. Then the students could return for the rest of their schooling and the younger children were accepted into the 2nd grade. It wasn't popular at first, but John stuck to the plan and under his leadership the compound school went from 170 to over 600 with another 5000 students in classes in the surrounding churches. And most important, hundreds of people were led to the Lord through the students' ministries.

The Campbells were at Durame for 7 years. Their family now numbered 6 with the addition of Carolyn, Charis, Samuel and Daniel. However, due to Marje's health, the family had to return to the states in 1964. John was pastor of a church in California for five years and then moved the family to Michigan where he was a regional sales manager for Zondervan until 1983 when he and Marje returned to Africa, this time to Liberia. They worked on the Firestone Rubber Plantation establishing churches and mentoring men and women. Some 43 churches were planted before war chased the Campbells home. When they were unable to return to Liberia because of continued fighting, they settled in Atlanta, GA ministering among the 30,000 Africans living in that area. The Campbells retired to Sebring the beginning of 1996 and John became involved in ministry in the local county jail doing what he loved to do, telling men about Jesus and mentoring them in their walk with the Lord.

John learned hard work as a boy on the farm and continued to work hard for his Lord all his life. He never would pass up an opportunity to share Christ with anyone, anywhere. He was focused on ministry and sometimes forgot that there were others that had a schedule that he had forgotten about. He could relax and enjoyed greatly working on a puzzle or playing a table game. John's health was slipping even though he still insisted things were okay. It reached a climax when he was admitted to the hospital due to his inability to function. There wasn't a clear diagnosis and he was discharged to the nursing home from where our merciful God took him home Saturday afternoon, March 3, 2012. John's story is concluded with a quote from his testimony that he wrote when applying to SIM in 1950: "I believe that the greatest job for anyone to do is to lead a soul to Jesus Christ. I thank God for the privilege that He has given me of leading many to Him. I deserve no credit and no glory for anything I have done. God deserves all the credit." This sums up John's life attitude.

Before Mr. Campbell came to our area only a handful of my people received teaching in grades one through four. Under his leadership academic education became available for the masses including me.

I attended kindergarten at Kajele Kale Heywet church school. Kajele is the name of my village where my mother still lives. The very first day our teacher asked the class to raise their hands if we wanted to accept Christ as our personal Savior. Without any understanding of what I was doing I raised my hand and accepted Christ but I had no idea what it meant to my life and my eternal destiny.

After finishing kindergarten at Kajele I went to Mishgida Church School for grades one through four. In that school Bible was the main subject. In grade two I learned about the saving power of the blood of Jesus Christ, the reality of heaven and hell, and that faith in the finished work of Jesus was the only way to heaven. Then, with understanding, I received Jesus into my heart.

Starting on that very day the Lord gave me an amazing

passion for Him and His Word. I began to read my Bible during the day and at night, and I started praying as part of my daily routine. I began preaching the Word of God in my village and my local church four years later. The more I read and preached the Word of God the sweeter it became to me and I began to obey the teachings of the Word in my daily life. God used those early years of my schooling as the foundation to my spiritual journey.

Early on in my Christian life I remember wanting a copy of God's Word like children want a coveted toy. This desire of mine for the Bible was a strong motivation to do well in school. By finishing first or second in my class I received a New Testament and some books which really helped me grow spiritually.

Grades five through ten were an even more pivotal time in my life because I entered the SIM School at Tezza. I never will forget that day in grade five when I finished first in my class and was awarded the entire Bible! It was the most thrilling day of my life. After that, my Bible became my closest companion.

In addition to that, SIM missionaries from America and Australia like the David and Luci Mai, Miss Warhanik, Miss Gibson, Mr. Nord, Mr. Nelson, the Zabels, Mr. Letcher, Mr. Jongeward were my academic and Bible teachers. They contributed a lot to my academic and spiritual growth. The foundation they gave me enabled me to pass my twelfth-grade government exam. Three hundred students from our area took the exam and only seven passed. Most of the students who passed were my classmates at the SIM School.

I want to say a few things about Mr. Mai and how God used his life to challenge me. He was the director of our school as well as my biology and chemistry teacher in ninth and tenth grades. God gave me the opportunity to learn from his commitment to God in his daily life and ministry. He invited me to a one-on-one Bible study on Saturday mornings in his office, which I did. His God-fearing life, his devotion and loyalty to God's Word and his energy in serving the Lord and others were extremely challenging and motivating to me. He gave me a guide for reading through the Bible in a year which I successfully followed.

In 1974 communism suddenly took control of our government. Many active Christians including myself became the targets of persecution by the atheistic communists. The missionaries were forced to leave the country including my spiritual mentor, Mr. Mai. It was a huge loss for me and I felt alone and helpless. You have already read about that time in my life in Chapter One.

The Durame Teza school as seen from the Ambaricho Mountain

The school compound from the front

Students raising the flag at sunrise before school starts.

Desta and other academic school students with their teachers

Durame Teza Mission Compound, SIM missionaries who taught at the academic school and Bible school before the eviction by the communist government in1976

John and Nancy Zebal, my
History and English teachers.

David and Luci Mai with Scott
their 1st son. David was my
Biology and Chemistry teacher.
Luci taught Geometry

Betty Warhamic, mu Geography
teacher

Chapter Seven

The University And My First Job

"Stay down! Stay down!" calmly whispered my devoted friend Elias Handiso. He was feeling anything but calm! The market place was crawling with communist cadres who were looking for me! Elias knew he had to appear calm and nonchalant in order not to attract the attention of those seeking my arrest.

As soon as two days after my unexpected release from prison, the cadres in my local area were again looking for me. I had avoided arrest during the twelfth grade by staying away from home and always walking on secluded back roads and paths when it was necessary for me to go someplace. I spent most of my time that year locked in my room studying or being inconspicuous and maintaining a low profile at school.

It was the first year for the Ethiopian School Leaving Certificate Exam (ESLC) to be administered in Durame. It is a rigorous examination taken over the course of three days. Those smart enough to pass were awarded a full scholarship to the university in Addis Adaba.

Because I was expecting death or imprisonment, I was not that anxious to see my results. I waited until the afternoon of the second day after the results came out to learn that I was one of seven of my 300 classmates who passed the test. That was when I began to be open to the idea that it was God's will for me to continue my education. Before that, I considered being an itinerate evangelist, but God was now telling me that this was not his timing for me to go into full-time ministry.

I went to Soddu Hospital, the only hospital in the region, for my physical to enter the university. It had been a mission hospital before it was taken over by the communist government.

Having passed the ESLC and my physical, I returned the 38 miles to Durame and had boarded the minibus headed to the university in Addis Ababa. My wonderful friend, Elias, who wanted to keep me company on that journey to start a new chapter of my life, was desperately trying to remain calm. The communist cadres were going from person to person asking, Are you Desta?!"

Suddenly, the driver started the bus as the cadres scurried off to check other buses. It was as if the driver all-at-once realized he was behind schedule and had to rush away in an attempt to get back on schedule. We were on our way!

Life in the university was much different than I had imagined. To tell the truth I was a bit apprehensive about entering the university fearing that my professors would try to indoctrinate me with atheistic ideology. But, in fact, the university became a place of refuge from those in my home area seeking to imprison me. My professors were completely immersed in the subject matter of my physics major. There was no time for communist indoctrination.

Though there were many students in my dormitory, I found a bathroom that had been abandoned because of plumbing problems, which became a prayer room for me. Surprisingly, there was another Christian student who was also looking for a secluded place to pray and who discovered that same room. Sisay Belete and I became best friends and prayer companions throughout our time in the university.

Because the university campus was huge with many wooded areas it was not hard to find safe places to study and to read my Bible and pray. I continued the program of reading through the Bible in a year throughout my time in the university. This proved to be a great source of encouragement to me as well as preparation for future ministry.

While I was in my second year of university studies I was again considering leaving my studies for full-time service. But again, God directed me to complete my university training.

During my four years at the university I served in various capacities in the Fellowship of Christian Students. I served as Bible study leader, Bible study material producer and prayer group coordinator. Even though we did not have freedom of worship on campus, the underground worship services were very active.

It was a time of spiritual growth and transformation in my personal life. God taught me a lot from my interaction with students from different parts of the country and church backgrounds. I was from a conservative church background, but I learned to integrate with and love those with a charismatic, Pentecostal background. Also, God began to give me a burden for people from ethnic backgrounds different from my own as I associated with these brothers and sisters from different cities and localities. God poured out in our hearts incredible love for one another so much so that I can say we were reliving the life of the early church in the book of Acts.

My time at the university was a time of spiritual growth broadening my mind and helping me to be accepting of others. It was then that I understood the reason God did not allow me to quit my high school and university studies. I can say that it was at this time that I came to see the beauty of the body of Christ. This laid a strong foundation for my future national and global ministry.

I was soon to discover there was another reason for my

university studies. I graduated with a Bachelor of Science in physics and was assigned to be a physics instructor in one of the Ethiopian government's administered teacher training institutes located in Bale province in the town of Robe. There were no evangelical churches in Robe at that time. Bale Robe is more than 250 miles southeast of Addis Ababa in the heart of the Oromo people group which numbers 40 million, the largest people group in Ethiopia.

Shortly after arriving at my teaching post I continued my habit of fasting and prayer on Wednesdays and Fridays. I began this practice with my friend Taddesse Yohannes in 1976 shortly after Mr. Mai and his family left Ethiopia. Communism was becoming more entrenched and the persecution of Christians more wide-spread. As we felt the erosion of our human support system we were driven to depend on God. God sent the fire of persecution, which led us to fast and pray.

Having learned the value of earnest prayer in knowing and doing God's will, I would have been the biggest fool to put a stop to this activity. Sure enough, God began to work. I like to say, "When we pray God works and when we don't pray, we work." Approximately three months after arriving in my new home, God brought a Christian named Zeleke Binchamo to me.

There were no churches in Bale Robe at that time, and Christians were few and far between. I have no idea how Zeleke heard about me except that he is a member of the neighboring people group to me and belonged to the same denomination. He was transferred from another part of Bale to Robe town. Zeleke is a strong Christian. Earlier in his life he had been bitten by a rabid dog. By the time he was able to get to medical help it was too late for the shots to help. He was sent home to die. However, the church prayed for him and God miraculously spared his life.

When he came to my house, Zeleke told me that he had heard

about me and wanted to join me in prayer for the evangelization of that area. That was the beginning of a wonderful partnership. We worked together for nine years. God blessed us in starting seven strong, praying churches in the Bale region.

During my time in Bale Robe, God blessed me with my marriage to Zenebech Oushe. We also formed a fruitful partnership in the Lord's work. Though we and a handful of Christians with us became the target of the Communists in the area, God gave us wisdom in how to establish churches and worship services underground. Our home became the main gathering place, and the beginning of the first church in town.

The external pressure caused by communism resulted in extraordinary prayer involvement. Weekly, we had two days for prayer and fasting, overnight prayer, two to three hours of individual prayer daily, and two hours prayer before our Sunday worship service. On top of that, we had many informal prayer meetings. Prayer brought revival. Churches were established throughout the province. Thank God that the church which was planted in our home during the early 1990s has grown to more than one thousand members and its influence is felt in the region and even the entire nation. Originally, when the government assigned me to Robe TTI, I was not happy with the assignment. Now I understood that God took me there for His divine purpose--sharing the gospel and planting churches.

God really used Mekonnen, my oldest brother, during my time at Robe TTI. He was not a committed Christian at the time but knew the peaceful, cooperative nature of my church denomination throughout his childhood and youth. Also, he was informed and very influential in communist circles. Mekonnen got wind that the government was planning to close the young churches that we had started in the area. He went to the officials of the area and spoke to them on our behalf saying that these people have no intention of forming an uprising against the government and that they are very cooperative and productive in the government development program. In this way he successfully interceded on behalf of these fledgling churches.

On another occasion Mekonnen learned of the government's intention to arrest me and put me in prison. Again, he went to the officials and told them that he was very familiar with the church denomination that I had been a part of from my childhood. He assured them that the denomination was peaceful and cooperative with the development programs of the socialist government of Ethiopia. At that time, he was the vice-commissioner of the audit department for Bale province and the officials could not risk embarrassing him by putting my wife and me in prison. Because we were the main leaders among the Christians in the area, God spared all the Christians from imprisonment by using my brother as a mediator.

God definitely used Mekonnen as a means of deliverance and protection for us His children on these two occasions. In addition, God used another means to deliver me from danger. Students often came to Robe TTI from all of Bale province as well as another neighboring province known as Arsi. Every year I formed an undercover fellowship of Christian students. Everything went smoothly for my first three years but during my fourth year a problem developed. A student who was committed to the government found out about the fellowship of Christian students and reported us to the communist leaders. They appointed informants to infiltrate our group and, only then, discovered that I was the initiator of the fellowship. They made plans to arrest me. I left for my home area on a certain Monday at the end of the school year for my wedding. Two days later on Wednesday the communist officials arrived at my house to arrest me, but I was gone. When I returned three months later everything had settled down and the officials were no longer looking for me.

Another way God supernaturally worked to turn a potentially disastrous situation into a positive situation was when God gave me favor with the principal of Robe TTI. There were three changes of principals during my tenure there. The third principal seemed to eye me with suspicion from the time he arrived. Perhaps he had been told to keep his eye on me by his communist superiors in the government. Be-that-as-it-may, one day during break I was sitting at my lecturing table on my stool with my physics books spread out on the table in front of me and on top was a Christian periodical I was reading. Out of the corner of my eye I noticed the principal enter the room. As he made his way to where I was sitting, I rearranged the things on the table so that the magazine was out of sight. He asked me what I was doing, and I answered that I was preparing for my next class. Without further comment he went to the back of the room and seated himself to observe me as I taught.

Later that day the principal called me into his office. He said, "Desta, I have been wrong about you. Now I realize that you are a hardworking teacher. I am going to award you with a two-week vacation." From then on, we were good friends.

As I look back at my years in Robe TTI, I am reminded of the Psalm that says, "Many are the afflictions of the righteous, but the Lord delivers him out of them all."

Chapter Eight

Romance and Family

Because of the difficulties of being a Christian under a communist regime, I lost all hope for a normal life. There was killing everywhere and the slogans we heard day after day were horrific. The stories I read about communism in Russia, China, Bulgaria, Romania and Cuba and the kind of suffering Christians faced shocked me. Reading about the history of communism in other parts of the world such as Wurmbrand's *Tortured for Christ*, discouraged me. And, too, because of what we had been experiencing in Ethiopia for the preceding five or six years, I had given up the hopes and dreams I had for my life. I even decided not to think about marriage because I did not want my wife and children to suffer because of my long imprisonment or death.

However, as I was finishing my university studies, God changed my mind. Because the intensity of persecution against the church was loosening a bit, I began to pray for the right girl to marry. I prayed for a girl who would not only be my life partner but also share with me as a ministry partner. As I was praying God brought Zenebech to my mind. She was the lovely girl I had known and fellowshipped with for seven years when we were members of the Mishgida youth choir. I mentioned her previously. She was the one who considered me a mature Christian brother whom she trusted with her questions about life and the Bible.

When I began to investigate the situation with Zenebech, I learned that she was being pursued for marriage by twelve young, rich and prominent men. They had been introduced to her by family and friends. What chance did I have being just a poor student? Thankfully, being rich and prominent were not prerequisites of this special woman whose heart matched her beautiful face. Her two main requirements and her prayers to God for her prospective husband were: "God, I want to marry a man who has a heart for God and a man who is more educated than I." She did not want to struggle submitting to the person who would be in authority over her.

Shortly after I started praying in earnest about this matter, we unexpectedly found ourselves together at the Tezza mission compound where we had attended school. She confided in me that she was having trouble deciding what she should do about marriage since she was being pulled in many directions. Unknowingly, I added to her confusion by revealing to her that God had given me peace about getting married, and that I wanted to request permission to pursue her in courtship and marriage. She was shocked and became totally silent to the point that we could not pursue the subject any further that day.

Subsequently, I wrote a letter to her explaining in detail how God had worked in my life to break down the barrier against marriage. I also told her how I had settled on her as the woman whose hand I would seek in marriage. My verbal request and the letter I wrote to her led her to complain to God that He was making the marriage question very complicated for her. God answered, "How am I making it complicated for you? You asked Me for a man who has a heart for God and who is more educated than you. I have brought Desta to you. He fulfills these requirements exactly! What are you complaining about?"

God used this reasoning and the encouragement of an aunt to flood Zenebech with peace and joy in her decision to accept my proposal. This aunt told her, "Zenebech, God's hand of favor is on

Desta. I believe he will be a wonderful man for you to marry." Now, I can say, there were two very happy young people who were deeply in love and committed to each other and to serving God together.

This however did not mark the end of the challenges we faced before marriage. That was Easter of 1982. We were married on July 14, 1987. During the more than five intervening years I finished my university studies and got established in my career. Zenebech stayed at home serving the Lord and looking for work. After more than two years of unfruitful searching, Zenebech found a secretarial training school in Goba, a town about seven-and-a-half miles from Robe Teacher Training Institute. Being close to each other during those almost three years before our marriage was both a blessing and a challenge. We were totally committed to a life of purity before marriage but we felt we should not marry until Zenebech finished her training and had worked a year in her profession. That's what God enabled us to do and we thank Him for His enabling.

When our first daughter was born, we named her Diliab which means, victory of God. Truly our God had defeated all the forces of evil that had threatened to disrupt our lives. Our next daughter we named Yadidiya which means, beloved of God. After that we had three sons: Eyoab - Jehovah is Father; Samuel - God hears; Eyosias - Jehovah helps. Our children have been a great blessing to us and we thank God that each one has a good name in the community. We are a close-knit family and we speak into one another's lives for the good of each member. Even the parents can receive a rebuke if need be.

I am so thankful for my wife, Zenebech, especially for how much wisdom God has given her in the upbringing of our children. I am always away for ministry so all of the responsibility for our family lies on her. She bore all the challenges of bringing up our children, family administration, government documents and dealings, and work in the local church.

God has blessed our children with amazing character and spiritual life. All of them are in leadership positions in the youth ministry of our church and in universities where they have attended and are currently attending.

Let me say a few things about my children. All of them are blessed gifts from the Lord. My oldest daughter, Diliab Desta, finished her undergraduate degree at Jimma University and is doing her graduate degree at the same university. She married a godly man named Alemayehu Atomsa. He is a graduate of the same university and a professor as well as an administrator. Diliab is serving in Emanuel Church of Jimma as worship leader.

Our second daughter, Yididiya Desta, graduated from Woleyita University and married a godly man named Asebegn Abute. Yididiya. She is working as a health officer at one of the health centers (mini-hospital) as a diagnostic doctor. Her husband has his own clinic. Both of them are very active members of the church in their town. My son, Eyoab Desta, has his undergraduate degree from Asossa University with high distinction. Currently he is on assignment. He is an amazing man of God. My son, Samuel Desta, is in Komolcha University and is majoring in electrical engineering. My last son, Eyosias Desta, is doing his Microsoft degree in Addis Ababa University. God has given each of my children and their spouses a heart for the ministry of AIPM.

Desta's family

Chapter Nine

Dark-Skinned People Can Be Missionaries

During my time at Robe TTI, while traveling back and forth from Bale Robe to Durame to visit my parents and relatives, God gave me a special burden to pray for revival among my people. That led me to start prayer groups. In 1984 during my summer break God's Spirit moved me to start this program in my local church and churches in the vicinity. Because this program spread and grew so quickly it became known as a prayer movement. The Holy Spirit was at work in the lives of many young people who were hungry for the Lord--zealous to see the lives of people transformed and to see a visible visitation of God. The movement was mushrooming in the whole region of Kambatta. God continued putting a heavy burden on my heart. I slowly began to realize that God was paving the way for revival.

With the communists being chased from Ethiopia. there came many changes, one of which was the restructuring of the education system. The new government decided to use the local dialects as the medium of instruction in its TTIs. That meant that all classes at Robe TTI would be conducted in Orminya. At that time, the government department of education transferred all instructors who, like me, were in places where we did not know the local dialect.

Even though I was given the opportunity to go to other more desirable places, I chose to teach physics at Durame High School in my home area. At that time, Durame had no electricity, clean water or even a house to rent. Yet, Zenebech and I knew that was where God wanted us to go. Being obedient to His leading in our life resulted in blessing for our future ministry.

Immediately, after my transfer to Durame, God gave me many open doors to travel and preach throughout the whole region of Kambatta, specifically speaking on prayer. Most of my audiences were youths whom God later used to bring revival to the entire region. God gave me a deep love for the youth and an effective strategy to impact them and enlist them for service in the Kingdom of God.

God also gave me an effective strategy for how to establish sustainable prayer groups in each local church. I spoke in more than 250 churches in Kambatta. Interest in prayer broke out like that of the Welsh revival of 1906. Every place was changed into a place of prayer, and all ages--children, youths, adults and the elderly became prayer warriors.

In the beginning the church leaders were not happy because the things happening at every church were new and different. Soon, however, their attitude became more positive. There was a new move of God's Spirit. People were openly repenting of their sins. Drug, alcohol and cigarette addicts and those who had other addictions were being liberated from their addictions by the power of the Holy Spirit. Many people made a covenant to fast and pray one or two days a week and to pray for one hour a day. This brought an incredible revival to each village, town and local church, and it birthed the prayer movement on Mount Ambaricho in the early 1990's.

At this time, I was approached about being appointed to a high government position. Initially I was pleased to be considered for this prestigious position but the Spirit of God impressed on me not to accept the offer. I declined the offer and continued teaching physics to my eleventh and twelfth grade students.

I had worked as a teacher in Durame High School for three years. It was 1995 when God gave me peace that He had heard my many prayers and that the day for me to go into full-time ministry had arrived. I will try to make a long story short about how God made His will known to me, and how He changed my thinking and ministry.

It all started in the hearts of two MKs (missionary kids) who had grown up in the homes of Ralph and Doris Jacobson and Gus and Lois Kayser on the Tezza Mission Compound. Tim Jacobson had returned as a missionary to Ethiopia after completing his schooling. God worked in Tim's heart showing him that the time had come for the Ethiopian church to have training for those God was calling out of the church for missionary service. It became evident that such training was necessary because of the challenges faced by those who had already gone as missionaries.

At the same time, the other MK, John Kayser, had been appointed principal of Bethany School of Missions in Singapore. BSM had been established by Bethany Fellowship International (BFI), a mission's organization in the United States whose purpose was to partner with third world churches in training their missionaries. Tim had stayed in contact with John and now approached John about the possibility of sponsoring two Ethiopian church leaders. These two leaders would receive schooling in how to train and send missionaries.

The BFI board approved this plan, and soon a search was underway to find two qualified candidates. A letter was sent to all the church areas throughout Ethiopia to give the local churches equal opportunity since all churches would be included in this mission's enterprise. When it was presented in my church the Spirit of God really moved me to pursue this opportunity. God used my time at Robe TTI to encourage those making the selection at the national level to select me. Because of the seven churches God had enabled my friends and me to plant during those nine years, the selection committee felt I was one of the ones God had prepared for this important work.

Now I had a decision to make. Was it really God's will for me and my family to leave the security provided by my teaching position for a life of dependence on the Lord to provide our needs? I have to confess that it was not an easy decision. As I reflected on all the ways God had proven Himself to me - He spared my life, provided my needs, and had allowed me to be selected by the church leaders for this training - I felt it was safe to conclude that this was His will. The peace in my heart allowed me to resign from my teaching position and move my family to Addis Ababa to the Evangelical Theological College (ETC) for six months of training before proceeding to Singapore. By that time I had four children, so it was no small task getting everybody settled in a new home. Thank God my wife and children adjusted quite easily to their new environment! The next test was much harder. At the beginning of the application process to go to Singapore, my understanding was that my family was included in the scholarship. Sadly, the school (BSM) told us that the scholarship was only for me and did not include my family. This information brought great distress to me and my family, especially my wife. It was one of the darkest times in our lives. Both I and my wife had resigned from our jobs when we left Durame.

Now I began to see the strong character of the woman God had given me as my life partner. My career as a trainer and sender of missionaries would have been aborted before it started if it were not for Zenebech's faith and fortitude. We went to God in prayer and my wife reapplied to her previous job. She was reinstated in a week's time!

Still her monthly salary was very small compared to our family's needs. It was not even enough for house rent let alone feeding the family and other expenses. To solve that problem my wife decided to stay with my parents who lived in a rural setting. My children had become accustomed to life in the city and my wife found it difficult to walk 40 minutes to and from work, so she sent the children to her sister and she decided to stay with my three cousins, Tessema Fote, Teketel Worku and Alemita Somano who were still single and had a house together. After two months, Tessema, who had built the house, gave a room for my wife and children. Can you imagine what it was like for ten people from different backgrounds to live under one roof? My three cousins already had two other people living with them. I will always be indebted to my cousins for their kindness to my wife and family during this difficult time. I don't know what we would have done without them.

Through all of this my wife never once complained about me resigning from my job or my departure to Singapore for my training at BSM. She has always been supportive of my ministry. Even after the completion of my course in Singapore, I traveled a lot for my ministry, so I was often away from home. Zenebech always tells my children about what a wonderful ministry "your father has." It is a blessing for me to be married to a woman who has a great heart and passion for the Lord and His work.

During my time in Singapore, because of the bond we shared through our common background with my people group, Dr. Kayser and I formed a lasting friendship that would be greatly used by God in my future life and ministry.

After my graduation from BSM with a Master of Arts in Intercultural Education, God brought me back with conviction, vision, passion and a burden for missions--spreading the good news of Jesus Christ to the lost both in Ethiopia and beyond her borders.

The following tells how that happened in my life and how it changed my direction.

While I was studying in Singapore all my classes were very challenging spiritually speaking. I was dedicating myself to the Lord repeatedly almost every day. The most challenging to me was my "History of Missions" class. I was hearing and reading the biographies of missionaries who labored tirelessly and sacrificially because of their love for the Lord and the lost people of the unevangelized nations of the world. I learned how some of them sacrificed their own lives and the lives of loved ones in the continents of Latin America, Africa and Asia. Their commitment, sincerity and boldness in sharing God's love for mankind, as well as their prayer life, really challenged me. After hearing and reading about these pioneer missionaries I rededicated my life again to God for the two primary calls in my life: prayer and missions!

In that class I saw the video "Peace Child." It told the story of Don Richardson and his wife Carol and their seven-month-old baby who went to the Sawi tribe in Dutch New Guinea in the service of Regions Beyond Missionary Union. I learned that the Sawis were cannibalistic headhunters. The Richardsons lived with them in virtual isolation from the modern world and were exposed to malaria, dysentery and hepatitis, as well as the threat of violence day after day. It made such an impression on me that I cried before God for the whole day! Also the biographies of Adoniram Judson to Burma, Hudson Taylor to China, William Carey to India, David Livingston to Africa, John "Praying Hyde" to Pakistan and a few others totally changed my attitude towards prayer and missions to the extent that I made a covenant with God to dedicate my life to missions, -- taking the Gospel to the lost and mobilizing churches for global missions.

After the completion of my studies in Singapore, my heart was burning with a passion for the lost, especially the Hindus of India. I began to pray for an open door to be a missionary there even for a short term. Miraculously, God answered my prayers.

God used SIM Missionaries Howie and JoAnn Brant to change the thinking of the Ethiopian Church especially Kale Heywet, my denomination, toward missions. Howie's parents, Albert and Evelyn Brant, had evangelized the Gedeo people group in southern Ethiopia, so Howie was raised in a missionary family as a missionary kid . When communism came to Ethiopia, Howie, who by then had returned to Ethiopia with his wife JoAnn, was involved in church planting among the Gurage people group. The communists came to their compound and marked all their belongings including their car POE (Property of Ethiopia) and sent Howie and JoAnn trekking to the nearest public transportation and back to their country. Then in 1990, even before the end of the communist era, Howie had come back to Ethiopia to visit the Christians in Gurage. During that visit he not only learned about the condition of the church in Gurage but also the condition of the church throughout the entire nation of Ethiopia. Though he was blessed by how the Lord had preserved the faith of the believers, he was concerned by the loss of their evangelistic outreach. He challenged the EKHC leadership to again become involved in sending missionaries to the unreached people groups of Ethiopia. This brought a mission movement within Ethiopia.

Howie returned to Ethiopia again in 1996. This time JoAnn was with him and they challenged the church in Ethiopia to send missionaries to India. The Brants chose southern India because of the compatibility of skin color and spicy food, and also because SIM had established an office in that area.

God used this partnership of the SIM and the Brants with the leaders of EKHC(Ethiopian Kale Heywet Church) to answer my prayer to go to India as a missionary. I and nine other Ethiopian men were chosen to be sent with the Brant's to India. EKHC paid for our expenses in India while SIM paid the airfare. By the grace of God, using door to door evangelism, 1357 people came to Christ during our two and a half months there. Until this time I and my people believed that to be sent as a missionary to another country you had to have white skin. Now we knew that God could also use dark skinned people as missionaries. Another thing God did during that short term missions trip to India was to establish a lasting friendship between the Brants and me.

Upon returning to Ethiopia, God opened many doors for me to travel all over the country of Ethiopia under the joint sponsorship of SIM and EKHC to do research with regard to the unreached people groups and to train and mobilize Ethiopian churches for missions. The more I spoke on missions the more I grew in my passion to live and/or die to take the gospel to those who have never heard.

After those four years of itinerant ministry, I was assigned by EKHC to be the Ethiopian director of Word for the World (WFW), a Bible translation organization headquartered in South Africa. Though I received a good salary from WFW I felt uncomfortable being in a Bible translation ministry because it was not my calling. At the end of my first year there I turned in my resignation to WFW in order to start Ethiopian Kale Heywet School of Missions (EKSM) at Durame Tezza, the first missionary training school in Ethiopia.

With the help of Dr. Kayser, my principal and teacher in Singapore and my friend, I designed the curriculum for EKSM. The instruction philosophy was KNOW, DO and BE and the training lasted for two years. The KNOW Phase included 25 missiological classroom courses studied during the first year. The DO phase was ten months of field experience doing evangelism, church planting and writing a practical research paper of what had been learned in the classroom and on the field. The BE phase was training in earnest prayer, personal Bible study and interaction with others in the classroom, dorm life, and group Bible study and prayer. Mondays were for prayer and fasting. In addition to this there were three days of prayer and fasting monthly and daily corporate prayer 5:30-6:30 AM and 6:00-7:00 PM. Graduates thank EKSM for giving them the opportunity to learn how to pray and do missionary work in a very effective way with saturated prayer.

Dr. John Kayser, who had grown up as the son of Gus and Lois Kayser on the Durame Tezza Mission Compound, is a godly man who has been mightily used throughout the world to develop missionary training schools. He was the founder of Bethany School of Missions in Singapore. God has used him greatly helping us in the establishment and operation of EKSM especially during its early stages. Each year he traveled to Durame to teach. He also recruited teachers for the mission's courses. God used him, Tim Jacobson and Howie and Joann Brandt to develop the church in Ethiopia into a missionary sending church. They invested a lot in the lives of people like me in time and resources and influence.

It is very important for me to acknowledge Bethany Fellowship International (BFI), a mission-minded organization which has sacrificed for the commencement and continuation of EKSM. If BFI was not involved EKSM would not exist.

Also, I want to acknowledge SIM. It had the vision for a missionary training program for the Ethiopian church in order to send competent missionaries within the country and outside Ethiopia. I want to also thank the Ethiopian Kale Heywet church leadership which had the vision for training Ethiopian missionaries for national and global mission work.

Therefore, the development of Ethiopian Kale Heywet School of Mission and the missionary training journey of my life is the joint effort of the many people and organizations whom I have mentioned above who have tirelessly and sacrificially invested in the cause of missions.

Dr. Howard Brant and his wife Jo-Ann

Dr. Howard Brant, teaching future missionaries

Chapter Ten

Reunited

Who was this man God brought into my life during my formative years and how did he influence me? I will use the following account to answer this question.

DAVID MAI'S STORY

A young teacher, David Mai, and his wife, Luci, were headed for Addis Ababa, the capital city of Ethiopia. It was Christmas-time 1969. David and Luci had been assigned to serve under SIM, then known as Sudan Interior Mission, an interdenominational faith mission with a lengthy history in Africa. As this young missionary couple boarded a Boeing jet for the long flight to Africa, they were buoyed by the prayer support of many interested relatives and friends, including ten churches and thirty-three individuals committed to be their monthly financial supporters.

The vision that had motivated them through the rigors of months of preparation and raising support was that of teaching Ethiopian youth about God's Word and God's world. They were unaware that God had been preparing a group of African believers with that same vision. They soon would discover that Ethiopian Christian families placed an equally high value on learning God's Word and on an academic education. In fact, not only is Bible taught as a subject in the church and mission schools, but many Ethiopian Christian young people take time off their academic training to attend Bible School. The young missionary math and science teachers were welcomed with open arms and found many ministry opportunities during the eight years they would serve Ethiopia before the Communist takeover would force the SIM missionaries to leave.

The beginnings of the call to be a missionary to Africa for David began in his boyhood days growing up in a Christian home in inner city Philadelphia. His father, Bill, had a passion for God and a burden for the salvation of souls. Weekly meetings were held in the Mai basement for the youth in their inner-city neighborhood. Games were played in one part of the basement and chairs and a podium were set up in the other. At first, guest speakers were invited to share the gospel message with the youth who attended but as Bill grew in his knowledge of God's Word, he became the regular speaker.

A machinist by trade, the godly dad and lay minister took a job in the Electrical Engineering Department of the University of Michigan. The family moved from Philadelphia to Ypsilanti, Michigan. The neighboring community of Plymouth had no local church, so Bill and a good friend who was a musician rented a tent and held evangelistic services intending to start a church. David, though only six years old at the time, always went with his dad to these Sunday afternoon evangelistic services. Normally the focus of the young lad faded in and out, but on one of those afternoons' things were different. Seized by a fear of death, David heard the words of eternal life through faith in Jesus' sacrifice for sin. The Holy Spirit caused the message to resonate in his mind. When his father gave the invitation the machinist's son walked to the front and prayed to receive Christ.

A couple of years later, when David was eight, his dad answered the call into full-time service to rural America with a home missionary organization called Village Missions. Though Bill had been offered the position as head of the machine shop which would insure the finest education for his children and a very secure future, he knew that God was calling him into full-time ministry. So he made a bold decision to leave the security of his job and follow the guidance of the Lord as he understood it. Afterward, David's grandfather told his dad, who was an only child, that before he was born the grandfather had promised that if God would give him a son he would give that son to God! David's dad was greatly encouraged by that revelation.

To follow God and uproot his family was not a one-dimensional, easy decision. The machinist's wife, Kass, David's mother, who greatly influenced her young son for missions by reading missionary biographies to the family, had dreamed of settling down close to her folks in Philadelphia, raising her family and living happily ever after. The move from Pennsylvania to Michigan had been an aberration to her dream. But she, too, sensed the call of God to the West and rural America. The couple pulled up roots and settled with their three children in the farming community of Foothills, some twenty miles northeast of Spokane, Washington.

Their new home was a parsonage on a homestead in the country where David grew up a farm boy instead of a city boy. It was a happy, busy life. There were several buildings on the self-contained homestead to explore and act out all kinds of imaginary situations. And there were also farm animals to take care of: a cow to milk morning and night, two beef calves, two 4-H sheep, several rabbits and some chickens. Everywhere he went his faithful companion, a dog named Laddie, was at his side. Two of the farmers in the community called on the young boy's services. A neighbor, Farmer Maier, came on foot across several fields with a cow for David to milk and thus, no more doing dishes! This friend taught David how to drive a tractor and how to haul hay.

Another neighbor, Herb Jacobsen, hired him to hoe weeds in his fields of grass seed. Herb had an older man working for him and

David and the man became close friends. The days and long rows of grass seed passed quickly as the old man entertained the boy with true life stories from his past.

Next, when David was 12, his dad, the Village Missions Pastor, moved his family to the farming community of Broadbent near Myrtle Point, Oregon. There David worked for many of the farmers gaining valuable life-skills and funds for college. Life-long friendships were established and life was good.

Just before David's junior year of high school, the family moved to the alpine town of Skykomish, east of Seattle in the heart of the beautiful Cascade Mountains. David was not happy to be moving from Broadbent, leaving behind the teachers, coaches and friends he valued so much. But his mother had comforted him with these faith-filled words, "Our disappointments are His appointments." David's disappointment melted away in the warmth of the natural beauty all around Skykomish and the question asked by Mr. Rhoads, the school superintendent and teacher at the local high school. "Are you a basketball player?" Mr. Rhoads explained, "Basketball is a passion in this town. It is the primary pastime for the kids here who start playing in the first grade. On game nights the gym is packed with all the townspeople as well as the skiers who come down from the slopes to spend the night in our hotel and motels and are looking for some good entertainment. Our teams are always competitive and fun to watch." That struck a very responsive chord in the future missionary who loved basketball.

One of his first nights in Skykomish there was a knock on the door of the parsonage. Five or six of the young men from the high school who would become David's classmates and teammates were at the door inviting him to go to the local café for a coke and to get acquainted. From that night on David felt at home in his new surroundings. He was learning that God is trustworthy and good, knowing his interests and developing his skills!

Before long David was a senior in high school and then went off to college. Another move brought his Village Missionary father back to Oregon to the coastal town of Langlois. The community church his father served as pastor for six years participated in a yearly round-robin missions conference. John Herr, Northwest Representative for SIM, was the featured missionary who presented the need for teachers to teach children of the national church that was being raised up in Africa. God was working as David came home for spring break of his senior year of college to work in Dick Tucker's sawmill, a job God provided for him during the school breaks. His dad shared with David the things he had learned from John Herr, including the need for teachers. This was all David and his wife needed to convince them that they should apply to become missionaries with SIM.

Going back to his time in Skykomish, God gave David a desire to teach a Sunday School class. This provided the first opportunity, as a high school junior, for him to teach elementary school children in his father's church. During his college years he taught the high school class in the church he attended. God used these and other opportunities of ministry and witness to confirm His call on David's life for ministry and missions.

His first teaching job was as a chemistry and biology teacher at Sunset High School in Beaverton, Oregon. As a first year teacher he requested and was granted permission to show a Moody Science film to his classes. After its showing to one of his chemistry classes, an outstanding student named Steve Simon asked him, "How do you know that the Bible is the Word of God?" Recognizing this question as evidence of the Holy Spirit's working in Steve's life, David began an ongoing dialogue and relationship with this student. Not only did they discuss what it means to be a Christian, but their mutual love of basketball and tennis led to shared times of recreation on those two courts. After a year or so, the teacher invited Steve to the Billy

Graham movie, "For Pete Sake," in which the gospel was clearly presented. Afterward they talked in Steve's driveway. When asked if he would like to receive Christ as his Savior, Steve answered, "I would like to do that." Steve's whole future changed and he eventually served as a staff member of Intervarsity Christian Fellowship for ten years and then the pastorate where he is still serving. The following is a note written by Steve to David nearly 40 years later.

"We hope you're doing well and that 2007 is off to a great start for you! We're digging out from a blizzard that cancelled church services today (Feb. 4)! Sure makes me miss the Northwest. We think about you far more than we communicate. I am so grateful that you introduced me to Jesus, Dave! I can't imagine what my life would have been like without Him! So, thanks for reaching out to that young high school kid so many years ago!"

After teaching three years in Beaverton, David and his wife headed for Ethiopia in December 1969 where they were assigned to teach for their first two years at Girl's Christian Academy in Addis Ababa. During those busy years these two young missionary teachers developed a real love for their students and staff and learned to like injera and wot, the national food.

After a brief furlough they were assigned to language school in Debra Birhan where they studied Amharic, the national language of Ethiopia, and Ethiopian culture. Halfway through language school they were blessed with the birth of their firstborn, Scott, who added a wonderful dimension to their lives and opened many doors for ministry. Following language school, the SIM Council assigned them to the recently opened Durame Secondary School established by SIM among the Kambatta Tribe.

While teaching Ethiopian young people about God's world as well as His Word, David encouraged his students and challenged them to do things that would help them grow in their Christian faith. One of his students, Desta Langena, took seriously every challenge whether it be attending group Bible study or a class on witnessing, a one-on-one study of John's Gospel or reading through the Bible in a year. Whatever the challenge, Desta embraced it wholeheartedly. Desta was not only a committed Christian, he was also an excellent student always ranking first or second in his class.

Since it was the custom of the missionary to visit the villages of his students and participate in church conferences or preach, Desta invited him to visit his village. He did this over a period of months, but David turned him down because of scheduling conflicts. Desta did not get discouraged but continued to invite the missionary. Finally, David had an open weekend. Seeing his student Desta on his home turf proved to be a great blessing. Desta was respected as much as any of the church leaders, though many years their junior. During the Sunday service, he interpreted David's message into Kambatinya, the local dialect. Before the weekend was over the student and his teacher had visited every home in Kajele, Desta's village. As they returned to the mission station after their visit to Kajele, David remembers thinking how greatly God had blessed him in allowing him to work with such special Ethiopian young people.

By that time, Communism was taking over Ethiopia. An Ethiopian young man named Mengistu Haile Mariam had been sent to Russia on a scholarship. He returned to Ethiopia, became an army general and with many of his comrades who had traveled a similar path, replaced Haile Selassie's benevolent dictatorship with Communism.

One of their techniques to disrupt the status quo was to turn the youth against those in authority. In youth meetings organized by the Communist Durge, the military junta that had replaced Haile Selassie, the youth were told that they no longer had to stand when teachers entered the classroom. This had always been the custom in

Ethiopian schools. The SIM teachers had tried to prevent the students from going to these meetings but Satan was at work bringing a spirit of rebellion on the land. Despite a valiant effort the missionary teachers failed. So, after returning from one of these youth meetings, students attending Luci's math class, all except one refused to stand to show respect. Desta took a courageous stand in front of his fellow students who were offended by his action. After the teacher left the room, one of them hollered out from the back of the room, "Desta, baa, baa, baa," inferring that Desta was a dumb sheep following its master. This was the most insulting gesture that could be made in this culture.

Not long after that, David and his family left Ethiopia for furlough and were not able to return because of the Marxist takeover which lasted seventeen years. Only months later all the missionaries were forced out of Ethiopia and the communist revolution was in full swing. (End of Mr. Mai's story)

Mr. Mai felt I should include the following letter that I wrote to him during the intervening years shortly before we were reunited.

LETTER

Dear Mr. Mai:

Greetings in the precious name of Jesus Christ our Lord and Savior. Here is a letter for you from your old spiritual son Desta Langena. Maybe you have totally forgotten me. I was your student at Durame Tezza SIM Academic School in 1971 through 1976. I was also working in your garden, and in the school. Much more than anything else I was your spiritual son. You taught me privately in Bible Study. You were weekly conducting a Bible Study program for me only. You have imparted so many spiritual blessings to me and your spiritual life style greatly influenced me throughout my life up to today. May all glory be to our God in Heaven forever and ever. Amen.

Whenever I think about you, unconsciously I began to shed my tears, because you were my spiritual model. Many times, I testified for many churches and even I wrote in my curriculum vitae that my life was mostly shaped by your biblical teachings and your spiritual life style as well as your commitment for ministry in order to expand God's Kingdom. Just a few months back I met Mr. Harold Jongeward, who is working now in Ethiopia as SIM Theological Education Coordinator. He told me many things about you. Mr. Jongeward was my 10th grade teacher of mathematics, immediately he remembered my face. Probably you can remember me if you see me again.

I heard bad news that your 1st wife divorced you. I am really sorry for that. I know that it was a very hard time for you to withstand such a difficult situation. But we believe that, for those who are chosen by God, everything can work all together for good.

I am happy that you have married a godly lady. Even though your ministry (mission field ministry) had been stopped, remember and know that the Lord is with you. If the Lord is with you, know that every place is a mission field. America is again becoming a mission field. We are seriously praying for America, Great Britain, Scandinavian Countries, Australia and New Zealand and Canada. From these countries all the 3rd world countries were blessed by receiving the good news. But today many of the churches are becoming empty, even some are closed because of materialism. I think the time is arriving that the 3rd world countries, have to send missionaries back to the western world.

Let me explain few things about my life briefly. I was your student in 9th grade in 1975 and 10th grade in 1976. After that, as you know you were obligated to leave the country (Ethiopia). While you were abroad, I wrote one letter to you and I remember you wrote me the reply. After that I joined the government academic school and completed 12th grade there at Durame High School. After that I joined Addis Ababa University and graduated Bachelor of Science in physics. After that I went to a place called Bale Region, which is spiritually very dark. But by the grace of God I stayed there for 9 years and planted 4 visible churches, and some other underground churches while serving as a government teacher there. Anyway, may all glory be to God our King Amen.

You know while I was your student, I got confirmation to be a full-time minister in His kingdom. But all the situations were not conducive for me to join any theological school. But after serious 17 years of prayer the Lord has opened the door for me, and I went to Singapore, Bethany School of Missions. I did my Master of Arts in Missions.

After my return to Ethiopia, I was moving all over Ethiopia, training pastors and churches, and mobilizing church leaders for world-wide evangelization. Just recently, Ethiopian Kale Heywet Church (EKHC) set up the missionaries training school at Durame-Tezza Compound. The EKHC assigned me as a Director of the College. By the grace of God I am directing the school. We have 32 students who are very much dedicated to God, enthusiastic and committed for missions.

Please, I am very much happy if we communicate periodically. Pray for me. Now I am the father of 5 children, and my wife is a dedicated, godly woman and she is greatly my help in ministry. May the Lord richly bless you and your family.

I look forward to hearing from you. Please extend my greeting to all your family members.

Cordially in Christ,
Desta Langena

Now, returning to my story, after my graduation from BSM in Singapore in August of 1996, I was deeply involved in ministry for ten years until 2006. My focus was preaching the Word of God in both urban and rural churches, teaching and directing EKSM and mobilizing churches for prayer and missions. This was the beginning stages of what was to become AIPM (Ambaricho International Prayer and Mission Movement), a grassroots missionary training and sending arm of the evangelical churches in Ethiopia.

In 2005 I began to pray about further education in missions. The EKHC leadership talked to me about getting a doctorate in missiology. When I asked if there was a budget for this they said, "No, but the Lord will provide."

God did just that! In April 2005 Bethany Fellowship International invited me to a missionary training conference in Minneapolis, Minnesota. After the conference I had an extra week before my return to Ethiopia. My wonderful friend, Dr. John Kayser, offered to buy an airline ticket for me to go anywhere in the States I wanted to go. Immediately I thought of Taddesse Yohannes and Mr. Mai out in Portland, Oregon. When I called Mr. Mai he was extremely surprised and pleased to hear my voice for the first time in twenty-nine years!

It was a joyous reunion when Mr. Mai and I met at Portland International Airport. Mr. Mai told me that seeing my face was like seeing Jesus face to face. We had a wonderful time of sharing God's faithfulness to each of us through trying times.

Part of God's purpose for that visit was to encourage this SIM missionary who had often wondered what had happened to his Ethiopian students. But there was another important part of God's plan and purpose for that visit which soon became evident. Mr. Mai communicated with Dr. Rick Calenberg, the Northwest Director of SIM about my visit and offered my services to him for sharing about the work of the church in Ethiopia. Dr. Calenberg contacted Scott Clark, the director of Worldview Center. Worldview Center was established by Dr. Donald Smith, formerly of Western Seminary, to house international students and their families while studying at Western and other institutions of higher education in Portland, Oregon.

I was invited to speak in the weekly vespers service to the students and staff at Worldview Center. As I was speaking the Spirit of God spoke to Scott Clark. He asked me to share any prayer requests . I gave four or five items related to my ministry at EKSM and the church. Scott was not satisfied to leave it at that. He probed further by saying, "We will pray for your ministry requests for sure, but is there any personal request you have that you would like us to remember in prayer?"

I revealed what the reader already knows about my desire and the desire of the EKHC leaders for me to get a doctorate in missiology. Scott asked his wife, Ruth, to take my requests to God in prayer. She prayed earnestly for me even shedding tears regarding my prayer items for my country, my ministry, my family and my future studies. I felt that the Lord heard the prayer of this godly woman. I sensed the presence of the Lord in a remarkable way.

After Vespers, while dining with the Clarks, Rick Calenberg and the Mai's, Scott told me that Western Seminary offered a doctorate in missiology. He also told me that they often have funds earmarked for training third world church leaders and recommended that I contact the president of Western Seminary, Dr. Burt Downs, with my need. Scott also told me that if I could get a scholarship to attend Western, that Worldview Center would give me a scholarship for my room and board.

Dr. Calenberg, who heard all that Scott had said to me, made a personal visit to Dr. Downs on my behalf. After hearing my story, the Western Seminary president graciously arranged for a full tuition scholarship for me to enroll in the Doctor of Missiology program at Western.

David and his family became my sponsors so I could qualify for a student visa. Along with the Mai's God used many others to provide my airline fare and to pay for my books and my living expenses. I am indebted to SIM International, Worldview Center, Howie and Joann Brant, Rick and Carol Calenberg and many others who sacrificially supported me financially during my three years at Western. I graduated on April 25, 2009 debt free!

Part of that three-year period I spent in Ethiopia doing research for my doctoral thesis, spending time with my family and caring for the ministries God gave me at EKSM and AIPM. AIPM by now had several missionaries serving full-time among the unreached people groups of Ethiopia.

God undertook for me in so many ways during this time in my life and I learned so many things about establishing and sustaining a missionary enterprise. When it was time for me to return to Western after several months at home I was praying about how to make that happen. At the same time I was praying, God prompted the Mai's to investigate where my program was and to find out what steps needed to be taken to get me back to the States to complete my program at Western. I am so thankful for this amazing answer to prayer!

When I completed my program and celebrated with my classmates and the many new friends God gave me during my time in the States, I prayed about and invited nine men to make up a board that would come along side AIPM Ethiopia in a fruitful partnership. That resulted in the formation of the AIPM USA Board. All nine men worked together for two years getting the ministry of AIPM USA off the ground. Rick Calenberg was the first board chairman and he along with Dr. David Stockamp laid the groundwork for a viable, effective operation producing a website, a DVD, and a brochure to present the ministry of AIPM to the body of Christ in America. Another board member, Mr. David Owen, created a "Join the Movement" card that God has used to mobilize a growing support team in the USA to partner with the soldiers on the ground in Ethiopia.

The Calenbergs have moved to Texas and other board members have had to resign from the board because of other commitments but the core of four members working with replacement chairman David Mai have sustained the ministry of AIPM USA which is now in its fourth year with two campaigns of about three months each when I have visited churches and home groups presenting the work of AIPM in America.

One of the instruments God has used in an amazing way is Stan Avery and the office of Unreached Villages which is housed in the home of Stan and Teresea Avery in Bandon, Oregon. Unreached Villages is a support ministry like the AIPM USA Board. They have been supporting the training and sending of missionaries in the country of India for twelve years. They have come alongside and mentored the AIPM USA Board as well as being the office which receives and transfers funds for the ministry in Ethiopia.

God used a critical connection to bring Unreached Villages and AIPM USA together. Stan Avery told David Mai, "You're Christie Lillie's uncle! Of course, we'll assist you!" The Avery Family and the Lillie family have fellowshipped and worshiped together for many years. Ben, Christie's husband, has been to India with Stan a couple of times. God uses relationships in building His Kingdom.

Can there be any doubt about God's involvement in bringing to pass this important fellowship between Unreached Villages and AIPM USA?! After eight years of working under the umbrella of Unreached Villages, AIPM USA has established its own not for profit organization.

Speaking of relationships this picture given by a friend to Mr. Mai's mother says it all. The caption reads: "Plans formed long ago with perfect faithfulness."

Mr. Mai, Desta and Mesfin

Chapter Eleven

A Prayer Movement Becomes A Missions Movement

When I returned to Ethiopia after completing my doctorate I was assigned by the leadership of EKHC to be the Director of Global Outreach. I served in that position from September of 2009 until November of 2011, approximately two years. During that time God enabled me to accomplish five important tasks. First, I recruited twelve missionary families. Second, I raised funds for these families to prepare them for global missions. Third, I thank God that most of them finished their training at EKSM. Fourth, these families have gone to the mission field. Fifth, I also prepared an 84-page manual for EKHC Global Outreach. It gave me much satisfaction to make these contributions to a mission-minded church like EKHC.

I resigned from that position not because of any conflict between EKHC and me but because of the very fast growth of Ambaricho International Prayer and Missions Movement (AIPM pronounced I-PAM). It needed my focused attention and full-time involvement.

Going back to how God led me to start AIPM I must take the reader to the time when I was imprisoned by the Communist regime. That was the time God taught me to pray. I learned the value of earnest prayer for my own spiritual life and also for my ministry. My involvement in the prayer band as a member and then the coordinator while at the university, as well as working with the underground church during the years of communist rule in Ethiopia were the experiences God used as His workshop for me. These experiences trained me and those I was involved with about the power of prayer. Robe City was one of the hardest cities in Ethiopia to live as a Christian and to share the gospel. Since prayer is the spiritual weapon that breaks down Satan's strongholds, we made prayer the number one activity of our life and ministry. We challenged those in our groups to commit to pray a minimum of three hours daily, fasting and prayer twice a week, weekly overnight prayer and a minimum of two hours prayer before any meeting or worship service.

Because of such dedication to prayer God rewarded us with many blessings. For example, when I arrived in Bale Robe in 1984 there were fewer than ten believers and there was no church. After nine years we had seen over 1,000 people receive Christ and churches established in different denominations. My denomination is EKHC. I and a few brothers and sisters started churches in Robe as well as in the surrounding towns which included Goba, Ali, Goro, Agarfa, Maliyu, Adaba, Gasera, and some other small fellowships. These towns ranged from 7 ½ miles to 62 miles from Robe. Each church experienced severe persecution from the communist officials but the Lord sustained His church and it increased in numbers. Currently, twenty years later, each church has more than 500 members and some of the churches have over 1000 members. All of them are involved in planting daughter churches.

I had been greatly burdened and praying for revival for my home area. Durame, a city of 50,000, is the largest city among the Kambattans, my people group. It lies at the foot of Mt. Ambaricho, the tallest mountain in southern Ethiopia at nearly 10,000 feet. God began to do amazing things. First of all, Abba Serecho, the 22nd generation witchdoctor, who was head over all the other witchdoctors in the area, renounced Satan and accepted Jesus as his Savior.

After my transfer from Bale Robe to Durame High School in 1992, the Lord placed a tremendous burden on my heart to promote prayer. I spoke in 250 churches in the area and formed prayer groups in each of these churches. In every conference where I preached, I focused on the responsibility of this generation to pray for revival. I gave special attention to devoted Christian youth and observed that some of them were already praying for revival. This confirmed to me that God was at work.

As a result, in the summer of 1991 revival broke out at the Tezza compound EKHC Church. Evangelist Tesfaye Gebre came to visit his in-laws. He had been praying for revival and God answered. Tesfaye conducted a one-month healing ministry at the church. Some who were part of that revival became key promoters of the yearly pilgrimages to the summit of Mt. Ambaricho to pray for world evangelization.

Though we do not know the specific date the first group went up to pray, it is agreed that there was a group of Christian young people, government workers, who came to visit their families during their summer vacation, who first went to the top of the mountain in 1989. Some from a neighboring community who observed that first group also started meeting for prayer on the mountain. These informal meetings continued for eight years by young people from different localities. I did a number of trips starting in 1994 with various choirs and prayer groups.

After many years of informal prayer gatherings on top of the mountain, God moved to bring about a united prayer movement starting in 1999. In December 1998, I went to India as a missionary with the team of ten Ethiopian missionaries as I mentioned earlier. While there I observed that almost all the mountain tops of India were full of Hindu temples. I realized that Satan wants the high places from which his servants can worship him. The May 28, 1999 gathering on the mountain was different in nature and size. Before my trip to India, I was attending the prayer meetings on Ambaricho. But this time I taught on the topic of prayer. Also, instead of it being a smaller, informal and more homogeneous group, it became a joint meeting made up of all the groups that had been going previously. This continued for four years. As I observed the fervency of the participants, mainly youths less than 25 years of age, and my passion for youth and the annual meeting began to increase. Also, the number of people in attendance began to double from year to year.

By 2003 there were 35,000 in attendance. That year something happened that God used to add a new dimension to the movement. My daughter, DilAab, my oldest child who was fifteen at the time, told me that she and four or five of her friends had been saving their money to buy snacks on the way down from the mountain. I jokingly suggested that they give some of the money for missions. To my amazement she agreed and gave me half of their money, fifty-two Ethiopian dollars. That sacrificial gift of those teenagers produced a huge struggle in my heart and mind. On the way up the mountain that year I wrestled with the Lord. "Lord, what should I do with this money," I asked."Send out missionaries," was His reply.

"Father, my people are poor. I can't ask them to do that," I objected. "You have been teaching about the wonderful things that have been accomplished through fervent prayer. Don't you believe what you've been teaching?"

Upon reaching the top of the mountain I found my wife and told her what had happened. We agreed to add one hundred Ethiopian dollars to the gift of DiliAb and her friends. I related the story to the conference audience and added that they could include their gifts with those already collected if they wished to do so. Those in attendance gave seven hundred Ethiopian dollars. The next year we collected six thousand seven hundred Ethiopian dollars! That was the year we sent our first AIPM missionary. On March 9, 2004 we sent Tamiru Langena, my youngest brother, to Sanbatte Shalla, a city of about 40,000 which was known as the Mecca of Ethiopia because it was a Moslem stronghold. There was no Christian church, and some who had tried to share the gospel there had been brutally treated by hostile Moslems. November 10, 2004, we sent two more missionaries, Getachew Mathewos and Kebede Helsebo to the mission field. Three additional missionaries were sent out in 2005. This, I can say, marked the birth of AIPM, and we became known as Ambaricho International Prayer and Missions Movement.

Our vision is to expand God's kingdom in Ethiopia and beyond by sending missionaries to unreached people groups which we have researched and targeted. Our objectives are mobilizing churches for world evangelization and church planting. We also recruit and train missionaries who are called to cross-cultural missions. And we create or develop partnerships with like-minded Christians, churches and organizations for the sharing of resources to advance the work of missions in Ethiopia and beyond.

God had prepared Ethiopian churches through persecution during the communist regime. He brought unity and spiritual strength to the body of Christ. Currently, the portion of young people in Ethiopian churches is eighty-five percent of the total congregation. These youth have an amazing passion for God, for ministry in the church and for missions work within and outside the country. The land of Ethiopia is like a Christian island in a sea of Islam. Which is to say, Ethiopia is surrounded by Islamic nations such as Sudan, Somalia, Djibouti, Eritrea, and even Pakistan and Iran. We have many Bible schools and one missionary training school for the training of missionaries. There are many local churches with a heart for missions. The Lord has brought the right time for the churches of Ethiopia to reach the unreached.

AIPM is directed by an Ethiopian board of interdenominational evangelical church members. The responsibilities of the board include recruiting and sending missionaries, preparing and implementing mission guidelines and communicating with churches and other partners by requesting and administering finances and making reports to the respective bodies. We also organize and conduct the AIPM annual prayer and worship meeting on Mt. Ambaricho January 19th every year. We also encourage like-conferences on the other 120 mountains in Ethiopia.

Annual AIPM Missions Conference

Prayer meeting on Mt. Ambaricho

Witch doctor who accepted Christ

Chapter Twelve

The Sanbatte Shalla Story

Sanbatte Shalla is a town of 40,000. It was called the Mecca of Ethiopia because there were no religious institutions other than the mosque there. All attempts to establish others were met with strong opposition and failure. However, God loves the people of Sanbatte Shalla and found someone who believed that if the light (Jesus) was made known that the darkness could not extinguish it (John 1:5).

In the beginning there was a Christian man named Ato Tura who was a trained nurse and ran a small clinic in this town. There had been many attempts to bring the gospel to this place. These attempts had gone on for three decades, but no one was bold enough to sustain a witness long enough for the message to take root.

Ato Tura was accepted in the society because he was known by many as their healer. He offered medical advice and sold medicine. He was able to exist there by being careful not to share his Christian faith. Attempting to do so would have resulted in his immediate eviction or worse. To maintain his faith in Christ, Ato Tura traveled 30 miles to Shashamane where he attended Sunday worship services.

In February 2004, two zealous EKSM students, Tagesa Tafessa and Kebele Hellsebo, were sent to the area for their one-month mission field experience. Before venturing into this Moslem stronghold, they spent three days of fasting and prayer asking God for the outpouring of the Holy Spirit on their ministry and for protection for their lives. As they entered the town they were immediately identified as Christian missionaries by the Moslem community and a riot broke out. The school had attained permission from the government for their students to do missionary work.

According to the Ethiopian Constitution there is freedom of worship and the right to share one's faith at any time and in any place. These students carried the documentation from the government giving them the legal right to be involved in their activity. This quieted the riot, but the Moslem leaders announced to all the townspeople not to associate with these men, and warned them to resist any attempts made by the missionaries to share their Christian faith.

Learning of this directive, the missionaries changed their strategy. They decided to fast and pray taking only their evening meal until they sensed God's guidance for direction to start the mission work. This went on for sixteen days during which Jesus began to reveal Himself to some of the townspeople who came to the missionaries secretly to confess Jesus Christ as their Lord and Savior.

Leaving their prayer chamber, they went out boldly preaching the good news of Jesus Christ to many people. Again, the Moslem leaders tried to start a riot but thank God the missionaries led twenty-three people to Christ and baptized ten of them after teaching them basic Bible doctrine. The baptism was conducted on the last day of their ministry, and during the baptism stones were thrown and many Christians including the missionaries received severe injuries. The persecution made the Christians pray fervently for God's protection over their lives and cattle, and for spiritual growth. The missionaries returned to EKSM to finish their training. What should the next step be to continue the work God had started in Sanbatte Shalla? That was my prayer.

I have two younger brothers, Abebe and Tamiru, whom I trained one-on-one, instructing both of them on prayer and missions. They responded positively to God's call to the mission field. Both had suffered persecution at the hands of the communists and were tried and true servants of Jesus Christ. Abebe and his wife Abebech went as missionaries to South Sudan for six years. Tamiru became the first AIPM missionary and was sent to Sanbatte Shalla, AIPM'S first mission field.

He graduated from Durame Bible School and attended the three year program at Soddu Bible College. While there he made a week-long visit to Sanbatte Shalla during which God gave him a great burden for the city. After his graduation from SBC, Tamiru was asked to become the senior pastor of his home church in Kejale but he told them the Lord was calling him to the work of missions and that he was volunteering to go to Sanbatte Shalla.

It was with mixed emotions that I received Tamiru's declaration. There was a good possibility that he could lose his life, but I realized that I must entrust Tamiru to God's care. Hadn't God preserved us during the reign of communism in our country?

Arriving in Aje, the town where the road to Sanbatte Shalla leaves the main road to Addis, Tamiru met Hussein Amman. He was the church leader in Aje and knew very well about the resistant people in Sanbatte Shalla. He cautioned Tamiru strongly, saying that it was very dangerous just to be known as a Christian in that town let alone a missionary. Tamiru delayed his journey for three weeks hearing the warnings of other church leaders and many other Christians.

As Tamiru prayed asking for guidance he had a dream. In his dream he saw hyenas mercilessly devouring the people of Sanbatte Shalla. Then he heard the voice of an invisible person speaking from heaven saying, "Unless you go and save these people, the hyenas will completely wipe them out." Calling to mind Paul's vision of the man from Macedonia, Tamiru received the assurance that it was God's will for him to enter this Moslem stronghold. He arrived in the town on April 1, 2004 and rented a room in Ato Tura's house.

It was Tamiru's habit to rise at 3:00 a.m. for prayer. The house next door belonged to one of the fundamentalist Moslem leaders. He heard Tamiru praying day after day. Then he hired some thugs to burn Tamiru's room.

At 2:00 a.m. one night the hired killers came and poured four liters of gasoline on the roof of Tamiru's room. On that particular day Tamiru was spending the night in prayer at another location but his missionary friend named Me'asso was asleep in his room. Then God did an amazing miracle. The fire burned on top of the house and rushed down the outside walls to the ground in a terrifying manner. Me'asso slept inside. The house, appearing to be engulfed in flames, aroused the attention of some Moslems who were up late and who because of the viciousness of the flames thought that this entire section of Sanbatte Shalla was in danger of burning down so they rushed to extinguish the flames. In spite of what looked like a horrible fire, there was no serious damage to the house, the room or Me'asso. Both Moslems and Christians marveled that the house and people had been spared.

On another occasion, 500 angry Moslems converged on Ato Tura's house where Christians were gathered. The roof was totally destroyed by the stones which were actually falling into the living room. Thank God that He protected the lives of everyone in the house. AIPM helped in the repair of Ato Tura's house. The aim of the attack was to kill the Christians and put a stop to God's work in Sanbatte Shalla. Instead it resulted in intensified prayer and worship of God by the Christians.

In March, 2005, my spiritual father, Dr. Howie Brant and his wife, Joann, came to teach some classes at EKSM. Howie was the SIM International Deputy International Director, SIM International. SIM is a missionary sending agency in the United States. Because of their heart for missions and for Ethiopia, as well as their fluency in Amharic, the national language in Ethiopia, Howie and Joann had been guest lecturers at EKSM since its inception. They wanted to visit Tamiru and the small group of believers at Sanbatte Shalla before they returned home. Since they were U.S. citizens, I felt it was safe for them to stop for a brief visit. However, immediately upon seeing the new visitors, many Moslems of Sanbatte Shalla surrounded the house the Brants had entered and began to throw stones. Though some of the stones hit Joann the authorities broke up the riot and the Brants were rushed away. Thank the Lord their lives had been preserved. However, now it was clear to everyone how serious these enemies of the gospel were.

In July, 2005, a man named Getachew Gensa and his devoted family gave land for a church to be built. They had been among the first to believe in Sanbatte Shalla. AIPM bought wood in Durame, which was 50 miles from Sanbatte Shalla. They had it delivered at night to the church site. Christians and missionaries from the surrounding area came together during the night and completed the building of the church in 14 hours. They started at 4:00 a.m. on July 30th and finished at 6 p.m. on the 31st. Only a little finishing work was done on August 1st. It was a miracle to us and to the threatening Moslems in the town. They were amazed at how committed Christians were to their faith and how the miracle-working God of the Christians enabled them to build the church in a single day.

Following the construction of the church building persecution of Christians increased. The town lost its status as the Mecca of Ethiopia because now there were not only mosques in the city but also a church. They were going to lose the money which they had been getting for many years from Saudi Arabia.

I believe that the attempts of the Moslems to destroy the Sanbatte Shalla Church and God's miraculous interventions give one of the most amazing testimonies of God's power to save His people in our generation. In November of 2005, during Ramadan, over 30,000 Moslems from the city and surrounding communities were gathered to celebrate. A discussion took place about how to eradicate the Christians from Sanbatte Shalla, especially the missionaries; Tamiru, Kebede and Getachew. The decision was made to kill some of the missionaries and the Christians. Thousands of Ethiopia dollars were collected to buy guns and bullets. The Christians prayed earnestly that their lives and the work of God in the city would be preserved. Government authorities were informed of the evil plans and arrested the perpetrators. Again, God had intervened on behalf of His people.

I want to share what happened to Getachew and his family. He was the man who donated the land for the church. His generosity to the work of the gospel brought intense persecution upon them. They considered him and his family responsible for bringing such shame to this respected Moslem community. His family became the main target for revenge. One hundred unknown people came to Getachew's corn field and destroyed it. His corn was all he had for food and cash for his children's schooling and clothing. It was considered a miracle that he was able to recoup 40 quintals (4 tons) from what was left behind by the destroyers. AIPM collected money from individuals and churches in Ethiopia and gifts were also sent from people abroad who learned about Getachew's trouble.

This happened two years in a row. When it happened the third year, Wizero Workie, Getachew's wife, shouted "Hallelujah!" saying, "Though the corn is fully destroyed in our cornfield, Jesus Christ is fully reigning in our heart!" This time Getachew had nothing left with five children depending on him. At the time I was in the States working on my doctorate. I shared the plight of this family with some of my friends and we were able to send $600 US dollars. Getachew was able to buy corn to feed his family and to pay his children's school fees.

Getachew also had cattle stolen. The entire family went to the AIPM Conference on Mt. Ambaricho except his wife, Wizero Workie, and their youngest child who was keeping the cattle. Two Moslem leaders tricked the child and took 3 oxen and 3 milking cows. The cattle were missing 7 days but Christians in Kambatta and in the area around Sanbatte Shalla were praying earnestly as the early church prayed in Acts 12 for the release of Peter. In the history of Sanbatte Shalla no stolen cattle had ever been recovered. But this time, as the result of earnest prayer it became known that the perpetrator of this crime was the son of the main leader of the local mosque and the one who called the Moslems to prayer five times a day. This became a huge shame for them, and the missing cattle were returned to Getachew. Observing such a miracle the Moslems of Sanbatte Shalla testified openly that "The Jesus of the Christians is great. Yes, indeed, the Jesus of Christians is great!" This created great awe on the part of the Moslems who brought a complaint to their leaders saying that they did not want to go to a prayer meeting led by a robber. The Moslem leaders terminated the prayer leader and hired another. This ushered in complete peace to the town and to Getachew and his family.

Some other incidents happened before this complete peace. In August, 2006 I visited the Sanbatte Shalla Church to say good-bye on my way to Addis Ababa to leave for my doctoral studies at Western Seminary in Portland, Oregon. I left my bag full of clothes with the driver of the bus. One of the prominent Moslem persecutors took the bag and disappeared. Thankfully, I had my travel documents, money and ticket in a separate bag I had taken with me.

After building the church, a fence was constructed with barbed wire and metal posts for its protection. At 1:00 a.m. one night hired criminals cut the barbed wire and uprooted the posts. Their plan was to enter the church, kill the Christians and destroy the church. Fifteen Christians were gathered at the time along with the missionaries Kebede Helsebo and Tamiru Langena. After the attackers broke down the door and entered the church one of the missionaries turned on his flashlight. God caused the light to have the intensity of stadium lights. The criminals fled for their lives thinking the government military troops had gotten wind of their plans and had set a trap to catch them red-handed. The light seemed to chase them as they made a hasty retreat.

The Ethiopian calendar is made up of twelve 30-day months. The extra days make up the thirteenth month, Pagume, of 5 or 6 days. These days are used by the church for fasting and prayer. By September 2006 the Sanbatte Shalla Church was a small but growing church of not more than 20 members. They were praying earnestly for God's protection rebuking and binding the spirit of destruction that was so prevalent in those days. It coincided with the 9/11 memorial in the USA. The enemy who had worked death and carnage in New York five years earlier was planning destruction and death in Sanbatte Shalla.

On September 10th the believers heard a rumor that the Moslems planned an attack on the church. Tamiru had gone to visit his parents. Kebede warned those gathered for prayer not to leave the church building because he had heard that anyone leaving the building would be shot. When the enraged enemies realized that no one was coming out of the church they decided to shoot through the church wall to kill the occupants. The first shot ricocheted exiting the roof. The second bullet came straight at the head of Kebede who had bent down to tie his shoelace, so the bullet didn't hit the intended target. The would be killers took a third shot, then left the compound thinking they had killed some of the Christians in the church. Thank God no one was killed or even wounded by those three shots.

On that same evening a Christian who had been severely beaten was at home alone bitter that he had been beaten. He cried out to God for relief from his pain, complaining that God was allowing him and the other Christians to suffer so much. It was the very time that the church was being shot at. Jesus appeared to his discouraged child and said to him, "I love you so much. I love the Christians at Sanbatte Shalla and all over the world. And also, you have to know that my blood was shed to save ALL sinners of the world including the Sanbatte Shalla Moslems. I love your persecutors, those who are giving you a hard time. Now stop complaining because of your suffering. Do not be discouraged or dismayed because I will never abandon or forsake you."

That was a great encouragement to him. Early in the morning he went to the church and met with those who had spent the terrifying night in the church. When he told them the message the Lord had given him, they rejoiced and immediately forgot their emotional pain and began to sing songs of praise to the Lord!

In March of 2006 about 30 Korean missionaries came to visit the church in Sanbatte Shalla. They had been hearing the news of the persecution and perseverance of the young Christians and wanted to encourage them. They arrived after dark and some Moslem youth quickly devised a plan to destroy the bus and take the belongings of the missionaries. They began by throwing stones and breaking out the windows of the bus. Then they forced open the door and as the missionaries were leaving the bus through the opened door the delinquent youths spotted two bags. They grabbed the bags and fled, obviously thinking they had what they wanted. Thank God that the missionaries arrived safely at the church. After entering the church they told us what had happened in town and that the two bags that were taken were full of garbage collected on the trip. The Lamb of God had pulled the wool over the eyes of the robbers. Again He protected the lives and belongings of His servants.

Another incident took place in April of the same year. I took about 30 people, a prayer band and other prayer partners from Durame to Sanbatte Shalla Church for fellowship and prayer. We had a wonderful time praying all night continuing through 3 p.m. the following day. When the bus came to pick us up for the return trip, we were not aware that a group of Moslem leaders had made a plot to intercept the bus and kill its occupants. Amazingly, as the group was ready to leave, a severe wind and rain storm came up suddenly and chased the plotters away. That group left the city without even knowing what the enemy had planned. It was like the days of Moses who crossed the Red Sea in peace and saw God sweep away the enemy.

From the time the church was built in Sanbatte Shalla the main Moslem leader repeatedly warned the Christians that he intended to shut down the church and chase the Christians out of town. In 2007 he himself finally left the city realizing that the church was not leaving.

Tamiru had been there for three years during which time there was much persecution and many attempts to defeat the work of God. During that time the Ethiopian government officials tried to put an end to these acts of violence against the church without success. In fact, the attacks seemed to intensify. Finally, however, by His divine means and favor God stopped the persecution and today there is peace between the Moslems of the town and the Christians. Church members meet freely in one another's homes without any stone throwing, yelling, beatings or threats of killing.

September 11, 2012 the Sanbatte Shalla Church sent its first AIPM missionary, and six other churches have been established in the area. The membership of the church has grown to 100. Our God is an awesome God!

Tamiru with Desta. The first missionary to Sanbateshalla

Getachew and his family the first converts and leader of the
church

The story of Sanbatte Shalla is being repeated in many other towns that are strongholds of Satan and his demons. The fearless AIPM missionaries are being empowered by God to break down these strongholds. As more missionaries are resourced more strongholds will be broken down. Since 2005 God has enabled these brave soldiers to see 6,000 people, every year, become believers and over 200 churches to be established as of 2018. AIPM USA is a channel God is using to deliver resources to this frontline ministry. If God has spoken to your heart through *Desta Means Joy* and you want to invest in this ministry you can reach us at:

AIPM USA
P.O. BOX 258
GRANGER, IN 46530

Phone: (574) 532-7177
Email: aipmusa@outlook.com
www.aipmusa.org

Dr. Desta Langena Letta

ABOUT THE AUTHOR

Dr. Desta received his first degree in Physics from Addis Ababa University and received his Masters of intercultural educations. in Missions at Bethany International University, located in Singapore. He received his Doctoral degree in Missiology from Western Seminary in Portland Oregon He founded and directed the Ethiopian Kale Heywet Missionary Training School for Missions in Durame, Ethiopia for 6 years prior to attending Western Seminary. After finishing his doctoral studies at Western Seminary he was assigned by the Ethiopian Kale Heywet Church to oversee all International Missions. All of these experiences equipped him to be a catalyst for the commencement and growth of the Ambaricho International Prayer and Missions Movement (AIPM).

Made in USA - Crawfordsville, IN
17184_9780578621869
03.25.2020 2051